Close Encounters of the Divine Kind captures the essence of my most desired experience as a human, and that is encountering and experiencing a loving yet supernatural God. The metaphors that are used in this book tell of the unrelenting pursuit we all follow to experience the heart of God. It may be disguised as scientific exploration and discovery or curiosity of unknown worlds and beings, but as is well expressed in this great book, we all have a yearning to encounter our Creator and be drenched in His presence. Ché Ahn tells us just how this is possible and how much this loving God also wants to encounter us more than we could ever fathom.

—MIKE BICKLE
DIRECTOR, INTERNATIONAL HOUSE OF PRAYER, KANSAS CITY
PRESIDENT, FORERUNNER SCHOOL OF MINISTRY

Ché Ahn is a gift to all who know and receive his ministry. His love for people, his proven pastoral heart, and his creative efforts at communicating imaginatively yet clearly to minds young and old alike have established him as a significant leader in many quarters.

—JACK W. HAYFORD
CHANCELLOR, THE KING'S COLLEGE AND SEMINARY
FOUNDING PASTOR, THE CHURCH ON THE WAY

Did you ever wonder why you are here anyway? Are you sick of religious answers? If so, you have the right book in your hand. Let Ché Ahn guide you through extraterrestrial realities toward fulfilling the exciting destiny that God has designed for you here on Earth!

—C. PETER WAGNER
CHANCELLOR. WAGNER LEADERSHIP INSTITUTE

D1550688

Dr. Ché Ahn is a master communicator who successfully takes on one of the greatest challenges imaginable in writing *Close Encounters of the Divine Kind:* he connects the purpose of humanity with the existence and nature of God. Thankfully, this book is not religious, yet it is deeply spiritual. The reader is drawn into a journey that will last a lifetime. *Close Encounters of the Divine Kind* will give wisdom to the one who is already a believer and hope to all who feel estranged from God's purposes for mankind. Read it, and join the adventure!

—BILL JOHNSON
AUTHOR, *When Heaven Invades Earth*

Prophetic communicators who see the dealings of God in more than the religious dimension are desperately needed today. Ché Ahn's new book is such a work—a bold wide-reaching look at our modern media's message through the eyes of a man of God. The real stars on God's stage are those who know Him and His world and are gifted to bridge the gap of the Fall for His glory. *Close Encounters of the Divine Kind* will help you see God's contemporary dealings with His creation in a whole new light so you can better fulfill His Great Commission. Read it and shine.

—WINKIE PRATNEY
AUTHOR, *Ultimate CORE: Church on the Radical Edge*

CLOSE ENCOUNTERS
OF THE
DIVINE KIND

CLOSE ENCOUNTERS

OF THE
DIVINE KIND

Ché Ahn
with Linda M. Radford

Charisma
HOUSE
A Strang Company

Most STRANG COMMUNICATIONS/CHARISMA HOUSE/SILOAM/
FRONTLINE/REALMS products are available at special quantity
discounts for bulk purchase for sales promotions, premiums,
fund-raising, and educational needs. For details, write Strang
Communications/Charisma House/Siloam/FrontLine/Realms,
600 Rinehart Road, Lake Mary, Florida 32746,
or telephone (407) 333-0600.

CLOSE ENCOUNTERS OF THE DIVINE KIND
by Ché Ahn with Linda M. Radford
Published by Charisma House
A Strang Company
600 Rinehart Road
Lake Mary, Florida 32746
www.charismahouse.com

Cover Designer: The DesignWorks Group, Charles Brock, www.thedesignworksgroup.com
Cover Image: Photos.com
Executive Design Director: Bill Johnson

Library of Congress Cataloging-in-Publication Data

Ahn, Ché, 1956-
Close encounters of the divine kind : intimate contact with God, the ultimate extraterrestrial / Che Ahn. -- 1st ed.
    p. cm.
ISBN 978-1-59979-072-5 (trade paper)
1. Theology, Doctrinal--Popular works. 2. God (Christianity)   I. Title.

BT77.A278 2007
230--dc22

                                              2007006210

First Edition

07 08 09 10 11 — 987654321
Printed in the United States of America

To my sister Chung-Hae Casler

And to my younger brother
Chae-Woo Ahn, MD (also a Trekkie):

I deeply love you and thank God for you.

ACKNOWLEDGMENTS

I am not a great speaker. I do feel that I am a good communicator. In the same way, I am not a great writer. But I do feel that I have communicated my thoughts well in the previous six books that I have written. In my inadequacies, God has always brought great writers to help me to polish my books. I will always be indebted to my friend Bessie Watson, who helped edit my first six books. But due to health reasons, she could not help me on this particular book. I was in a very busy season of my life and couldn't imagine how I could complete this project without her assistance. But then God sent Linda Radford into my life. Until recently Linda worked as a child psychologist, and a year ago she became a member of Harvest Rock Church, the church I am privileged to lead. She is also a very creative and gifted writer. She came into my life and into this book project at just the right moment. Amazingly, Linda always had a passion to write since she was a young girl, but she never had a book published. When I approached her to help me write this book, she prayed and said yes! Words are always inadequate to thank people who help make your dreams come true. But this time, this book is also a dream come true for Linda. Thank you, Linda.

I also want to thank Stephen and Joy Strang. I will never

forget the Charismatic Leaders Gathering a few years ago when I said that I should write a book for Strang Communications. You immediately pursued me and offered me a contract, not knowing what I would ultimately write. Thank you for believing in me and in this project. Thank you for allowing me to write this radical, unconventional book. I never dreamed how the Lord would meld my lifelong interest and enjoyment in science fiction with His own heart of love for lost humanity. In many ways, this book is the product of a series of downloads from the Lord in which He has presented Himself in a new parabolic form for our current age. He continues to amaze, astound, and delight me!

Finally, I have to thank my family, starting with my wonderful and beautiful wife, Sue. We will be married twenty-eight years when this book comes out. My children, who are young adults, Gabriel, Grace and Steve, Joy, and Mary, thank you for always supporting me as I write, travel, and pastor a great and wonderful church. Ultimately, I want to thank Jesus and want to give Him all the praise and glory for everything in my life. Oh, how I love Him so!

CONTENTS

CLOSE ENCOUNTERS WITH THE DIVINE KIND

Like many people, I love movies. My favorite type is the science-fiction action thrillers like *Star Wars*, which I saw six times as a kid in the theaters. I don't remember how many times I saw it on video and DVD. And I haven't missed one *Star Wars* episode that has been produced. I love movies like *The Matrix* and *Alien*, all of them with their sequels, which I have also seen numerous times. I will never forget seeing *Alien* when it first came out in theaters. I saw it in a new movie theater built with surround sound, which was the cutting-edge sound technology at that time. The special effects, the directing, and the cinematography made me feel that the alien was directly over my head in the rafters of the theater. To say the least, it scared the bejeebers out of me, and I loved every moment of it! Before you judge me for being a sick science-fiction freak, I want to make a point that I am not the only one who enjoys this type of film. In fact, these movies will go down not only as science-fiction classics but also as movie classics, period. Why? Because these movies and other science-fiction movies like *E.T. the Extra-Terrestrial* are some of the highest grossing films of all time.

The question is, why are science-fiction movies so successful year after year? I think there are several reasons. First is the obvious fact that these movies are well made and entertaining. Second, the continuing advances of computer-age special effects put the current movie industry on a whole different level than the science-fiction movies of yesteryear. (Even the original *Star Wars* special effects I loved so much then seem Mickey Mouse to the special effects of today.) But I believe there is another reason for their popularity.

These movies speak to certain needs that we all have about our purpose in life and about the future, and many of these movies have the dimension of the supernatural. These movies speak to the inner hunger that is within all of us concerning encountering another world, another realm—a spiritual realm. They may even give us hope of encountering a being from another world who is more powerful and wiser than we are—perhaps even the hope that "somewhere out there" is a "Messiah," a "Savior" (like Neo in *The Matrix*).

That is why *Close Encounters of the Divine Kind* was written. Using analogies from movies that have impacted our culture, this book tells the story that there is another world that is more real than this physical world. There is a real extraterrestrial who is alive and well, and anyone can have an encounter with this ET. It is an encounter of the divine kind. It is an intimate encounter with God, the ultimate extraterrestrial. And as much as I love movies and the special effects of Hollywood, a real encounter with God will transcend any movie experience you have ever had. It will change your life inside and out. It is an encounter that I experienced in 1973, and I have never been the same. It is a real encounter that will transform your life and your world. So if you are searching for truth and meaning, if you want purpose in your life, read on, and may you too have an intimate encounter with God, the ultimate ET.

∿(**1**)∿

WE ARE NOT ALONE

It **is early** evening as two people climb a solitary cone-shaped mountain. Reaching the flattened summit, they are able to look out over a rugged and deserted plain in this remote section of Wyoming. As they walk around a large boulder, they see that inside the top of the mountain is a well-lit, open area surrounded by viewing decks, loud speakers, cameras, and banks of mainframe computers. People in white lab coats and workmen in yellow hard hats are everywhere, and they seem to be anticipating something.

As everyone watches, several bright lights come together in the northwestern sky and move in their direction at rapid speed. Three eerie disc-shaped aircraft, each brilliantly lit, appear, stop instantaneously, and hover over the open area at the mountaintop. The people stop all activity and stare at the aircraft. They are fascinated, but no one appears frightened. A technician in a lab coat begins playing a sequence of five tones on an electronic keyboard that is broadcast through the loud speakers. The sequence is repeated more and more quickly. As if on cue, the three aircraft respond together with similar tones and fly away.

Everyone begins applauding. They shake hands and congratulate each other. Apparently they see this encounter as a successful attempt to communicate with the unusual aircraft. Looking up, the two observers see huge thunderhead clouds beginning to surround the mountain. Many brilliant lights begin flashing from the clouds, and multiple aircraft, similar to the first three, rapidly appear and surround the mountain on all sides.

Suddenly, a huge aircraft comes out of the clouds and flies over the mountain. It beams out tremendous light and a strong electromagnetic energy field. It too is disc-shaped, but it is multiple stories high, as large as the mountain itself. As the lowest section of the aircraft hovers over the open area on the mountain, all human activity stops. The technician plays the five tones over and over, and suddenly the huge craft answers with a blast of low tones that shatters windows on the viewing decks, sending showers of glass flying everywhere. For the next few minutes, the aircraft rapidly plays a series of tones, and the humans repeat them. This cycle is repeated again and again. It is communication through imitation, but the humans do not know what it means.

The huge aircraft stops playing tones and becomes very still. A hatch begins to open from the lowest section of the aircraft. As it opens, dazzling white light streams out. The people in white lab coats and yellow hard hats move back, but all eyes remain on the hatch opening. Slowly the silhouette of an upright body with a humanoid shape and thin insectlike arms and legs appears. It moves forward, but the bright backlight from the open hatch covers its face and features with shadows. As everyone watches, scarcely breathing, this first being is joined by several dozen smaller creatures with similar thin humanoid bodies, large heads, and spindly arms and legs. They stand facing the humans and appear to be waiting for something.

Men and women in orange jumpsuits walk into the open area between the humans and the strange alien beings. It is obvious that these are scientific volunteers, each willing to leave with the aliens. However, the aliens move to the end of the line, selecting only one human volunteer. They surround him on every side, carefully touching him as if they are fascinated. They gently guide him to the hatch opening. He pauses and looks back at the other people. Then he smiles with eager eyes glowing and willingly enters the aircraft with the aliens. The hatch closes, and the aircraft slowly lifts and flies away.[1]

Are We Alone?

If you saw the Steven Spielberg movie *Close Encounters of the Third Kind*, you probably recognize this description of the closing scene. This was an excellent movie in a series of Hollywood sci-fi flicks reflecting our interest in the possibility of contacting alien life. As a culture, we have a fascination with the idea of life somewhere else in the universe. On one hand we hear scientists discuss whether conditions essential to life as we know it exist somewhere else in our galaxy. We also hear news reports of people who claim to have seen UFOs or been abducted by aliens. These reports are imaginative and interesting, but the idea of being kidnapped by an ET seems a bit of a stretch for most of us! Still, many of us (50 percent according to a recent Gallup poll[2]) admit that we wonder about alien life forms elsewhere in the universe and think that they probably do exist.

In fact, some people are convinced that aliens have already visited Earth! They look at the massive stone structures of ancient civilizations such as the pyramids in Egypt or Stonehenge in England. It is still a mystery how these ancient structures were built using stones weighing many tons without modern construction equipment. Some people wonder if aliens visited Earth long ago and used their superior technology to personally direct the building of these monuments. Actually, several decades ago, in the early 1970s, a "pop science" book titled *Chariots of the Gods* by Erich von Daniken claimed that aliens have done just that.[3] Von Daniken looked at a number of complex structures and other objects (like the highly accurate solar calendar of the Mayans) from these ancient cultures. He concluded that there were a number of common features among them that provide evidence that these cultures may have been "tutored" by the same alien beings. This idea is probably more creative fantasy than serious science. But at the time, *Chariots of the Gods* captivated people's imaginations and sparked lots of debate about the possibility of extraterrestrial life.

Why do we have such an ongoing interest in the possibility of alien life forms? Is it the result of our scientific understanding of how vast the universe is? We now know our own Milky Way galaxy contains some 100 billion stars. Many of these stars may have orbiting planets like our own solar system. The vastness of the universe certainly suggests the possibility that other life might exist somewhere in all that space! Surely somewhere in all these potential planets there must be some other life! (Like maybe amoeba? Or moss? Or perhaps spores? Or what about little green men? Or the blob?)

But is it more than just the size of space that makes us feel we are not alone? Is there something else, something inside of us that compels us to believe there must be more than just us? If aliens visited Earth as von Daniken suggested, would they leave any "signs" of their encounter with us? Could that encounter leave us with an inner impression that there is more than the everyday world that surrounds us? That there is something or someone else "out there" and that we are not alone? Could this be a reason why we find thoughts of extraterrestrial life so intriguing?

The Ultimate Extraterrestrial

I believe that this is exactly what has already happened. We have actually had an encounter with a true extraterrestrial—but an extraterrestrial from another space, another time, another dimension, the ultimate extraterrestrial: God. This experience left a permanent impression on our collective human memory that we do not seem to be able to erase. The evidence that we carry this impression is everywhere. We are fascinated by super beings who are not bound by the physical limitations of normal human beings, and they come in every size and shape. This fascination begins as soon as we are old enough to hold our first superhero toy. Do you remember watching the Teenage Mutant Ninja Turtles or the Power Rangers? They could do superhuman feats of strength and skill, and we dreamed of being like them. Psychologists tell us that young children are captivated by their enchantment in superheroes because children feel small and helpless. They want to identify with someone they see as powerful and invincible. This explanation certainly makes sense when we are talking about children. But why don't we outgrow this interest as we get older, wiser, and more competent?

Our enchantment doesn't fade away. Instead it shifts to new images. I doubt you tune in to *Power Rangers* anymore, but when was the last time you saw a *Terminator* flick? Why do superheroes like Spiderman and Superman keep making successful movie comebacks with people of all ages? Our fascination with super beings is not new. In fact, throughout human history, all cultures have had ideas about super beings or deities who were more intelligent and powerful than humans. These beings were believed to control the forces of nature. To be safe and protected, you had to keep these super beings happy and on your side, usually by offering sacrifices. For example, the ancient Phoenicians believed that their god Adonis died each fall and was resurrected each spring by his lover Astarte, the goddess of fertility. Under this belief system the Phoenicians sacrificed to both these gods to insure the continuation of the planting and harvest seasons.

Clearly, religions based on these deities became extinct as science offered better explanations for natural events. Knowing, for instance, how tremendous electrical energy is generated in a thunderstorm does away with the idea that someone needs to volunteer to be lunch to calm down an angry deity who is hurling thunderbolts at us! Some people argue that scientific understanding does away with all need for religion. For them, religion is simply a set of superstitions that will in time, and with increasing knowledge, fade away. Maybe this is true, but we don't see it happening right now. Despite our increasing advances in technology, the majority of people in the United States believe in the existence of a supreme being, and there is a growing interest in spirituality of all types. A recent national survey of religious beliefs and practices indicates that in the United States, 70 percent of people believe in a deity they call "God," and 90 percent believe that some type of "higher power" exists. Additionally 60 percent of Americans say that they pray several times a week.[4] It appears that no matter how technologically advanced we become, we can't shake the conviction that there is "something more," something beyond the everyday world that our five senses experience.

Science and Reality

Many people reject the idea of a spiritual dimension or any spiritual deity as irrelevant, because its existence can't be scientifically proved or disproved. But perhaps we shouldn't be so hasty. The history of science contains many examples of things that were thought to exist before they could be scientifically proven. This was often because the right instruments to measure them did not exist or no appropriate experiment to investigate them had been devised. There are many examples of this in the history of science. For instance, let's look at the existence of bacteria as a cause for disease.

In the late 1600s Anton van Leeuwenhoek, a Dutch shopkeeper, used crude magnifying glasses and discovered what he called "little beasties" (actually bacteria) in a drop of stagnant pond water. These microscopic "aliens" were strange and fantastic creatures like nothing else ever seen before. Van Leeuwenhoek's discovery opened up a whole new dimension of reality, the invisible world of the microscope. His discovery produced interest in these "curiosities" but hardly set off a stampede of scientific experimentation. No one made links between the existence of bacteria and the possible effects they might have on other living things, like causing disease. The common knowledge of germs that confronts all of us every time we see the Wash Your Hands sign in our public restrooms was completely hidden from science for the next two hundred years! Although the existence of the microscopic aliens was a fact, no one had conducted appropriate experiments to observe their behavior.

Finally, in the mid-1800s, French scientist Louis Pasteur

did experiments that showed that bacteria were responsible for the fermentation process in yeast. In other words, bacteria could cause a biological process to occur in something else. Pasteur suggested that other types of bacteria might also cause other biological processes such as illness. The resulting germ theory of disease caused a radical shift in medical thinking about the study and treatment of human illness. You can blame Pasteur for all those hours in your life you've spent washing your hands!

Let's go even smaller. Everyone is aware that atoms exist and that everything is made up of atoms. But did you know that this idea goes back to two Greek philosophers, Leucippus and Democritus, who lived in 500 B.C., one hundred years before Aristotle? They suggested that all matter was made up of infinitely small, simple, and indivisible parts called atoms. The concept that everything is made up of invisible atoms intrigued scientists for centuries. But the work that demonstrated the existence of atoms and their structure did not occur until the scientific studies of Ernest Rutherford in 1909–1911.[5] He performed a series of experiments in which he bombarded gold beaten into a thin foil with positively charged alpha particles. At the time, scientists believed that atoms were a homogeneous glob of positively charged matter containing scattered negative electrons, sort of like pudding with raisins. To Rutherford's surprise, the alpha particles mostly went through the foil with no resistance. This phenomenon demonstrated that atoms were mostly empty space with a well-defined core or nucleus. Almost overnight, his work revolutionized thinking about the structure and behavior of atoms. Scientific thinking entered the atomic age.

The history of human knowledge and science has its blooper

hall of fame, too. Many ideas we once held to be accurate have turned out to be incorrect as scientific methods became more sophisticated. For instance, before the late 1600s people believed that life formed spontaneously, sort of mystically, through a phenomenon called spontaneous generation. Here's how it worked. You put a piece of meat out in the sun, leave it a few days, and suddenly maggots appear from nowhere. It was an observable and repeatable phenomenon, at least to the naked eye. So it must be that life generated out of nowhere, like a process of spontaneous combustion. (We know better, but let's not forget we have microscopes that can see incredibly small critters!)

Then, in 1668, Italian physician Francesco Redi discovered that if you put two pieces of meat in the sun, but covered one with a cloth in a glass container, only the uncovered meat would generate maggots.[6] This was an interesting finding suggesting something else must be happening, but no one was sure what it was. Well, of course, we know that the flies landing on the uncovered meat were laying eggs, which, though invisible to the naked eye, were responsible for producing the maggots. Then, a few decades later, van Leeuwenhoek (name sound familiar?) made his discovery of those "little beasties," or the world of microbes. Armed with this information, scientists eventually concluded that the laws of physics and chemistry, not mysticism, could explain how life regenerates. So nothing was spontaneously generating after all.

A more recent example illustrates how science changes its thinking over time. Until the early twentieth century, the universe was thought to be the Milky Way galaxy. Science believed the universe was held together by opposing forces of gravity, or what Albert Einstein called "antigravity."[7] Einstein thought this opposing antigravity force had to exist throughout space to keep the force of gravity from pulling everything together. This concept suggested a static universe in which everything was held in its permanent place. Then in 1919, Edwin Hubble began his studies on the Andromeda Nebula with the Hooker 100-inch telescope at the Mount Wilson Observatory in Pasadena, California.[8] What he discovered exploded the then known universe. Many observed nebulae were not stars surrounded by dust and gases, as formerly thought, but galaxies in their own right. The size of the universe was staggering! It was far vaster than previously imagined. What was more, it was not static but expanding! Hubble soon discovered that the galaxies were moving away from one another at the speed of light. Almost overnight the field of astrophysics was turned on its ear. A new theory explaining the history and beginnings of the universe was now necessary.

These stories from science should caution us. Just because at this time we have no scientific way to directly observe or measure a "spiritual dimension," we should be careful. We must not conclude that we will never develop the technology to do so. The further we push our understanding of the material world, the more the distinction between material and nonmaterial dimensions begins to blur. For example, take particle physics, the study of how subatomic particles behave. We now know that in empty space, such as outer space, these subatomic particles pop in and out of existence all the time. Where do they go when they are "out of existence," and where do they come back from when they pop "into existence"? We really don't know.

Or take recent evidence from astrophysics, the study of the

universe and its components. Until recently, the theory of the origin of the universe went something like this: The universe began with a cosmic explosion, or "the Big Bang" as it is called. Since then the universe has been expanding, but at a rate that is gradually slowing down due to the pull of gravity as it draws bodies of matter together. Eventually this process will cause the universe to slow to a stop and reverse or start imploding (be pulled back together). This process is called "the Big Crunch" and acts sort of like a giant cosmic trash compactor.[9] Of course, this process will take many more billions of years, so no one needs to lose sleep worrying about getting smashed!

But if you are a cosmic worrier anyway, there's good news! Recently we have discovered that this process is not happening, that quite the reverse appears to be the case. The universe is not slowing down, but is actually speeding up! This finding contradicts what we know about gravity and the way it works. There must be some other force in the universe countering gravity and pushing galaxies apart with increasing speed. It is a force unlike anything we have on Earth and has been named "dark energy," probably because we are literally in the dark about it. We have no idea what makes up dark energy or where it comes from. One theory is that it comes from apparent nothingness. We do know that the universe is not largely vacuous space as we once imagined. Instead it is literally teeming with far more energy than we can detect. And it is highly likely that two-thirds of the energy may be this "dark energy," a form of reality unlike anything we have on Earth and about which we know nothing!

Our expanding scientific knowledge reminds us that we must be careful. We must not get locked into thoughts about the world that may limit our understanding of reality. We can see histori- cally that some of our scientific thinking has turned out to be wrong. It is impossible to know how much of our current knowl- edge will turn out to be inaccurate in the future. It seems that the more we expand our understanding of the material universe, the more we bump into unseen and unknown factors and forces. These factors and forces defy all physical laws of operation we currently know, and they are impossible to measure with any instruments we've currently developed. Although we don't yet know what they are, we do know that these factors and forces must exist.

Could other dimensions of reality also be present just off our current scientific radar screen? If a divine ET, God, exists, might He simply defy all our currently known laws of operation and be impossible to measure with our current instruments? Might He exist outside our four-dimensional reality and yet be able to penetrate it and communicate with us? I believe that this divine ET does exist and that He has and is continuing to communicate with us!

Communication from Another World

Can you imagine the excitement that would result with a communication from another world? How might an ET attempt to communicate with us? Finding a common language could be a real problem. This communication problem was a major theme of the movie *Contact*. The main character, Ellie Arroway (Jodie Foster), is a researcher dedicated to scanning space in search of extraterrestrial intelligence. After several years of finding nothing, she and her colleagues stumble upon a patterned signal that is repetitive and intentional. It sticks out against the white noise of the background microwave radiation that fills outer space. They tune in to the signal and discover that it is a complex transmission of thousands of pages of numbers, an obvious communication from somewhere else. But they have no clue how to decipher or interpret the number code. Eventually they find the codebook primer hidden within the code itself and translate the communication. They discover that the code contains detailed instructions for building a transport machine, and a multinational effort begins to construct it.

The movies *Close Encounters of the Third Kind* and *Contact* are entertaining and imaginative speculations. Yet I believe that they are based on a dynamic tension within us that we cannot escape, a tension that keeps nudging us that we are not alone in the universe. Perhaps we even hope that other intelligent, far more intelligent, life exists out there and that our contact with it will open undreamed possibilities for us.

To receive communication from an ET and be able to decode and understand it would be an amazing discovery! To learn about "another world" or a "different dimension" would be totally fascinating to most humans. If it were published in *TIME* magazine, would you be curious to find out what it contained? Wouldn't you be willing to stand in line to get a copy?

Would you be surprised if I told you that such a document exists and is available in bookstores everywhere? It is called the Bible. It is, I believe, a true communication from the ultimate extraterrestrial—God. Jews and Christians alike believe the

Old Testament contains the thoughts of God, and additionally, Christians believe that the New Testament does as well. By any set of standards, the Bible is an amazing book. Written over a period of two thousand years, it contains sixty-six books penned by at least thirty-nine different authors. While not written to be a history book, archaeological finds continue to overwhelmingly support the Bible. Where contradictions have occurred, most have been resolved when additional discoveries were made. One famous example is the frequent mention in the Bible of the Hittites. This was a civilization totally unknown until about one hundred years ago when their capital, Boghazkoy, was discovered east of Ankara, Turkey.[10] Prior to this discovery, the Hittites were believed to be a Bible myth. But in the past one hundred years, archaeologists have uncovered a wealth of information about the history, language, and culture of the Hittites.

The Bible is also known as a prophetic book. A prophecy is a foretelling of specific events in detail many years, sometimes centuries, before the events happen. The Bible contains approximately twenty-five hundred specific prophecies, two thousand of which have already been fulfilled to the letter. Could this just happen by chance? Could someone just make two thousand lucky guesses? (This part gets a little mathematical, but try to hang in here with me.) Using methods of statistical probability, it is possible to calculate the odds that a prophecy is accurate by chance. Bible prophecies are generally independent of each other. This means the odds of all two thousand prophecies accurately predicting events without error due to chance is less than one in ten to the two-thousandth power.[11]

"So what does that mean?" you may be saying. "It's all

numbers to me!" Well, statistical odds less than one in ten to the fiftieth power are considered impossible to occur by chance. Let me explain. Let's take a globe the size of Earth and fill it with marbles, each the size of a pinhead. We put a special mark on one marble and throw it in with the rest. Now we give the Earth-sized globe a good shake. We blindfold you and let you pick one marble. Do you think you'd pick the marked marble on your first try? Probably not. In fact, you wouldn't be surprised if you never found that marble, would you? Your odds of finding that marble on your first try would be about one in ten to the fiftieth power. The odds of all the two thousand prophecies being accurately predicted are astronomically higher than this. This could never happen by accident. (By the way, congratulations for hanging in there. You just completed your first lesson in statistics!)

We can see, then, that it is statistically impossible that so many prophecies could have been accurately generated by chance. But what if those prophecies were given to human authors by a divine ET existing outside the fourth dimension of time who can see the future? Is this why they were fulfilled so accurately?

A side note: because the Bible is so frequently used by groups with a religious ax to grind, you may feel put off by the mention of it. I do not blame you. I wish it were not the case, but, unfortunately, the Bible is often used to promote all types of personal agendas. This results in so many confusing and conflicting messages that many people decide to ignore it altogether. But the misuse of the Bible should not prevent us from taking a good look at it for ourselves. Could the Bible be a message left for us by the divine ET? If it is, then the Bible must mean something. It must contain important information about and from the divine

ET that He wants us to know. Certainly an ET of such superior intelligence would not leave a garbled communication. Is there a codebook primer that we can use to correctly unlock the meaning in the message?

Theological scholars spend years studying Hebrew, Greek, and ancient languages trying to better understand the meaning of the Bible. But the Bible itself identifies the key to its own interpretation. It makes frequent reference to the existence of a primer, actually a personal coach or mentor—the Holy Spirit. According to the Bible, personal contact with the Holy Spirit will guide us to all the truth and open up the meaning contained in the message. And the Bible states that this type of firsthand contact is possible for everyone to experience.

The Bible is not a book that you read like any other book. It is a living communication that opens to you through intimate contact with the Holy Spirit. It contains information and instructions that will open the doors of your perception to another world, another dimension, another reality. I encourage you to obtain a Bible. Approach it with a sincere and open mind and heart. Let the Holy Spirit guide you, and you will find that portal to another reality.

About This Book

Obviously this book is about knowing God and having contact with Him. It is not about religion. I believe that God has encountered the human race in the past and is still involved in close encounters today. I know this because I have directly experienced such an encounter, and I know others who have as well. I believe that the divine ET has given us a powerful communication about Himself and another reality in His book, the Bible. Plus, He wants each one of us to enter into another dimension of reality through intimate contact with the Holy Spirit.

I don't expect you to believe me based on words alone. I do intend to encourage you to venture forth and seek your own "close encounter of the divine kind." I will point out some things I have learned and share some personal experiences that others and I have had. In the end, you will need to decide for yourself. If a divine encounter occurred in the past and communication was left with a tutorial coach, the Holy Spirit, then contact is possible. You can have personal firsthand contact with God, the divine ET, if you will pursue it.

This book is an invitation to you to have your own firsthand encounter of a divine kind with God. If you will sincerely seek this contact, I know God will respond and reveal Himself to you in a way you cannot deny. I believe that God desires to have such contact with every single human being.

In the movie *Contact*, Ellie Arroway takes a trip in the transport machine to another reality. However, when she returns, she finds she has no scientific data to back her experience. A scientific panel questions her about the accuracy of her experience. She acknowledges the lack of scientific evidence to prove it but states, "I can't [withdraw my story]. I had an experience. I can't prove it. I can't even explain it, but everything that I know as a human being, everything that I am, tells me that it was real. I was given something wonderful, something that changed me forever. A vision of the universe that tells us, undeniably, how tiny and insignificant, and how rare and precious we all are.

A vision that tells us that we belong to something that is greater than ourselves, that we are not—that none of us are—alone. I wish I could share that. I wish that everyone, if even for one moment, could feel that awe and humility, and hope..."[12]

Although spoken by a character in a movie, these words capture an experience that I believe is available to all of us in reality. I challenge you to read on. Actively engage in what you read, and anticipate a true encounter.

The following chapters deal with how to make contact. Step forward and go where you have never gone before. See if the divine ET, God, does not reveal Himself to you. See if you do not experience a living connection with the presence and mastermind behind everything we see and know.

⤛(2)⤜

FIRST CONTACT:
THE EDEN DIMENSION

If you had the ability, what changes would you make in the world? We might have different priorities for change, but virtually everyone can agree that the world could use some improvement. Some might put world peace at the top of their list; others might emphasize ending famine, conquering AIDS, providing more opportunity for minorities, or equalizing wealth or the political power structures. Still others of us might pick goals closer to home, like providing for the material needs of our family and friends. But none of us would have difficulty coming up with a list of improvements. It is safe to say that we can all agree that we live in a world that is less than perfect.

It may be hard for you to conceive of a being like a divine ET introduced in the last chapter just for this very reason. You may look at the world around you and wonder, "If a divine being exists, how can this being allow such imperfection to continue, especially when people are getting hurt and even dying! Surely the state of the world is proof that no such being exists! How could a divine ET condone all the suffering, oppression, and injustice that exist today? Especially if this being is powerful and can change things for the better, how can He just stand by and watch?"

This is a very important question to address. Let me do it by asking you to consider these questions: Why do suffering, oppression, and injustice bother so many of us? It appears they have been part of the human condition throughout recorded history. Why haven't we gotten "used" to these "realities of human existence" as sort of "normal"? Why, now and throughout history, has our species so frequently fought against suffering, oppression, and injustice in all its many forms? Why do we have a sense of frustration and a desire to somehow address these difficulties and make things "better"? What is this sense of "better" that we want to achieve, and where does it come from? And why are we so convinced that we can make positive change in the face of so much negative history?

I think that our discontent with our imperfect world suggests that we carry within us the understanding that things not only could be better but also should be better, and that our sense of achieving something better is connected to an ancient past when we experienced something much, much better than the world as it presently is. I think that this imprint of a more perfect world is permanently etched into us, along with the knowledge that as a species we have an important destiny. We have a purpose here.

Doorway to Another Dimension: Reading the Bible

In the last chapter I introduced the Bible as a communication from the divine ET. It contains information and instructions that will open the doors of your perception to another dimension of reality. The Bible gives us a description of the ancient past and how our world was radically different than it is now. If you have never read the Bible before, I want to encourage you to do so, because I want you to experience this information for yourself firsthand. So I challenge you to actively read the Bible. What I mean by "active" is this: approach the Bible with an open mind. Ask the divine ET to open its contents to you. If you do, it will "come alive" and begin to speak to you by inviting you into another reality.

Before we look at what the Bible says about the ancient past, I want to tell you a few practical things about how to read it. If you go to buy a Bible, you may get confused because you will find that there are many different types or versions of Bibles. These are different translations. Some, like the King James Version, were written hundreds of years ago and use a form of English that can be difficult to understand now. I suggest you try a modern English translation like the New International Version (often called the NIV). It is very readable. If your first language is something other than English, you may find a Bible written in your primary language easier to read. When people quote from the Bible, they usually tell you what version or translation they are using. In this book I will usually quote from the NIV. When I use a different version, I will identify it in parentheses after the quote.[1]

The Bible is organized into two major parts: the Old Testament, which has thirty-nine books, and the New Testament, which has twenty-seven books. Some books have more than one volume, so they are labeled 1 and 2 (for example, 1 Kings and 2 Kings). All Bibles have a table of contents in the front that lists all the books and the page numbers for each one. Each book is subdivided into chapters, and each chapter has verses or sentences that are numbered. So when you see a notation or reference like John 3:16, it simply means the Book of John, the third chapter, and verse number 16. Using this reference system makes it easy to quickly find any specific place in the Bible.

We are now ready to consider what the Bible tells us about the ancient past.

Eden: Our Original Home

Genesis is the first book of the Bible, and its first three chapters contain important information about our past. In these chapters the Bible describes a perfect place—a garden called Eden, which God created for us. Perhaps you have heard the story of Eden and Adam and Eve, a talking snake, and an ill-fated bite out of an apple. I'd like to revisit this story with you. There are differences of opinion on whether the story is literal or not. But for our present discussion, I believe our primary task is to focus on what the divine ET communicated in this story. Doing this will help us understand some important things about who He is and who we are.

When you read the first chapter of Genesis, you find it describes God as creating the earth. The Bible gives a broad outline of this process, not highly specific details, probably because the details would fill libraries full of volumes. Most important in this account is that God wants us to know that material reality was His idea, and He likes the material world and thinks it is good. As you read the first chapter of Genesis, note that as the material universe is unfolding, God is watching and approving it. For example:

> And God said, "Let the water teem with living creatures, and let birds fly above the earth across the expanse of the sky." So God created the great creatures of the sea and every living and moving thing with which the water teems, according to their kinds, and every winged bird according to its kind. And God saw that *it was good.*
> —Genesis 1:20–21, emphasis added

After the material world came into being, Genesis 2:8–14 indicates that God created a very special place for human beings, a garden called Eden. If you think for a minute, you realize that the fact it is called a garden indicates that it was deliberately designed. Gardens don't just happen. They are planned and planted. The Bible states that God put all kinds of trees in the garden that were good for food. Four rivers are named as flowing through it, two of which, the Tigris and the Euphrates, we know to this day.

It was an incredible place! Lunch was always available for the picking, with no extensive preparation time or any cleanup required! It appears that the environment was climate controlled, as clothes were not necessary. Imagine never having to check the weather to know what to wear! It even had its own built-in sprinkler system, for Genesis 2:6 says that "there went up a mist...from the land and watered the whole surface of the ground" (AMP). There were all kinds of animals to watch and interact with because they were tame and unafraid. (The fear between humans and animals is described as entering the world later. [See Genesis 9:2.]) Even the name *Eden* gives us a clue about the garden, for in Hebrew it means "delight" or "pleasantness." Eden was truly a perfect paradise, like heaven on Earth!

Eden: A Drama Epicenter

We all know that when there is an earthquake, there is an epicenter, or place of origin for the quake where the major slippage has occurred. The epicenter triggers slippage along a fault that causes the earthquake to radiate and its effects to be felt many miles away, depending on its size. Eden was a perfect paradise, but we don't see it anymore. Throughout human history, in our explorations and in our art and history, we humans have tried to find or re-create paradise. Remember Ponce de León and the Fountain of Youth, the stories of exotic Shangri-La, and the many failed attempts to create utopian communities? Today you can search the world over, and you will not find paradise. What happened to it? The Bible tells us that a major drama, a true tragedy of earthshaking proportions, took place in Eden and radically changed the entire world. Before we view this drama, let's take a look at its key players.

God: The Infinite Lover

There are not enough human words to even begin to capture a description of the divine ET. Picture for a moment the vastness of the universe with anywhere from 50 billion to 100 billion galaxies, each with 100 billion to 200 billion stars. Now think about the fact that all of them are moving away from one another simultaneously at the speed of light. Imagine a being so intelligent, with memory banks so large, that He can pinpoint the exact location of every star and is so familiar with each one of them that He identifies them by name! The Bible declares in Psalm 147:4, "He determines the number of the stars and calls them each by name." Now imagine, if you can, a being so vast that He not only can pinpoint the location of everything but also is able to simultaneously be everywhere at the same time! Psalm 139:7–10 describes God in this way:

> Where can I go from your Spirit?
>> Where can I flee from your presence?
> If I go up to the heavens, you are there;
>> if I make my bed in the depths, you are there.
> If I rise on the wings of the dawn,
>> if I settle on the far side of the sea,

even there your hand will guide me,
   your right hand will hold me fast.

This is an alien being unlike anything we can conceive!

And yet for all His vastness, nothing is too small or insignificant to escape the divine ET's watchful care. He is aware of the activity of every creature everywhere (Psalm 50:10–11). He knows the fate of every tiny sparrow that falls to the ground, counts the number of hairs on your head, and even knows exactly how many tears you have ever cried (Matthew 10:29–30; Psalm 56:8).

The Bible uses many words to describe the attributes of God, such as *almighty, changeless, just, merciful, faithful, ever watchful, comforting, protective,* and so on. But the single most dominant characteristic of God is love. In fact, love is so central to the essence of God that the Bible states that "God *is* love" (1 John 4:8, emphasis added). God is called the almighty Father and depicted as desiring a family. The Bible indicates that human beings are God's greatest creative act. He made human beings for union with Himself. Throughout the Bible the divine ET is pictured as pursuing and wooing the human race, in much the same way an ardent lover sticks to the one he or she loves. He wants to have intimate friendship with us and pour into us His resources of power, joy, peace, wholeness, completeness, prosperity, and wisdom. He wants us to long for His presence as He longs for ours. He seeks increasing intimacy with us. He wants our lives to be saturated with enjoyment of the riches and vastness of existence that He knows.

He originally intended that we would partner with Him in learning how to reign and have dominion over the earth. This was to be training for our eternal destiny: to be seated with Him and reign in heavenly places. We are creatures of significance and purpose, and He deems each one of us as having infinite worth and value. He wanted us to discover our uniqueness and personhood within a growing, expanding community of love with one another. No wonder the universe is created in such an expansive way. We were meant to fill it with the passion, joy, and creativity of our union and communion both with God and with each other!

lucifer: Darkness Disguised as light

Have you noticed that all our human dramas contain an essential conflict and an antagonist who is always a shadowy character? Without this dynamic tension, our story line seems to evaporate! Lucifer is the prototype for all our antagonists, for he was our first adversary and remains our most vehement enemy. He is also known as Satan or the devil, but his original name was Lucifer, which means "light-bearer." It is important to remember this name because it gives us a clue to one of the primary ways he operates. He makes evil look good, falsehood look true, and darkness seem like enlightenment. He is the ultimate deceiver.

Lucifer began well, in fact, very well. He was an angel with high ranking. Ezekiel 28:14 refers to him as the guardian cherub, or the cherub that covers. Apparently he was second only to God Himself in rank and power. Unfortunately his position inflated his ego, and he decided to lead a rebellion against the reign of God. Rebellion is a form of opposition and defiance motivated by pride. Although doomed from the start, Lucifer must have made a convincing argument, for the Bible states he was able to influence a third of the angels to join forces with him. (See Revelation 12:4, 9.) There was open rebellion in heaven, and Lucifer and the renegade angels were defeated and ejected from heaven. Most of this story is told in Ezekiel 28:12–19 and Isaiah 14:12–17; we will look at it more in depth in a later chapter.

Once ejected, Lucifer showed up on Earth, probably because he was watching God's project with humankind with great interest. The name *Satan* means "adversary," and from the beginning he is identified by the divine ET as our most persistent and dangerous enemy. (See 1 Peter 5:8.) Having lost his position, he may have been jealous of our appointed destiny with God. Or he may have been so angry and filled with hate that he wanted to continue to lash out against God in any way he could. Whatever the reason, the Bible indicates that we became central targets in an ongoing brutal assault in which Lucifer's primary activity is to steal from us, kill us, and destroy us (John 10:10). Since he is a constant liar (John 8:44) and very cunning (2 Corinthians 11:3), his favorite tactic is disguise and deceit (2 Corinthians 11:14). He prefers that humans do not even know he exists. It makes his destructive work against us easier to accomplish. He will always cloak his activity by hiding his true motives, and he is absolutely merciless (Luke 8:29). Anyone who thinks they are in a partnership with Lucifer in which they have any degree of control or safety is already demonstrating that they have been duped and are being played for a fool. Continued association with Lucifer always leads to personal ruin, self-destruction, or even death.

Human Beings: God's Eternal love Objects

Human beings stand out as distinct in the Bible account of Creation. The divine ET gives an extended description of our design and creation. At the end of the first chapter of Genesis, the Bible states that God does something very unique. He decides to make a creature in His image. The idea here is not just that He made a creature that bore a resemblance to Him. He created a being like Himself in both form and function (Genesis 1:26–28). In fact, we are told that God breathed His own essence, His Spirit, into our being (Genesis 2:7). We are such an essential and substantial representation of the divine ET that in our creation we were a visible representation and an operating manifestation of Him. If that mouthful sounds impressive, it should. It means that He created us to be able to have His authority and power.

The Bible makes it clear that both men and women were made in God's image and are coequal. They both were immediately given the mandate to subdue, replenish, and have dominion over the earth (Genesis 1:27–28). The Garden of Eden was a perfect paradise, but it did not cover the whole earth. Men and women were put on an earth that had experienced a cataclysmic destruction by a renegade, rebellious fallen angel, Lucifer, who had already set up a base camp. God's intention was that we would take control of the entire world and rule it. We were to fill the earth and wholly occupy it, and to come against and conquer any territory inhabited by Lucifer. Actually, we were given the authority to subjugate and rule over him and eject him from our domain, Earth, the same way he had been ejected from heaven.

God wanted us to grow and mature by exercising our rulership in this way. He wanted us to willingly choose to join Him in a ruling partnership in the heavens. We were created as His family and heirs to everything He has. Our destiny was nothing lower.

In this way, we as humans were to be like the divine ET who has dominion over all the universe. According to the Bible, God intended for us to be responsible for the earth, to protect and nurture it and use its resources wisely and well. He wanted us to take responsible rulership, and He truly released the dominion of the earth, its welfare and its future, completely into our hands. The Bible describes a particular instance of this. God brings all the animals to the humans to be given names (Genesis 2:19–20). This was much more than labeling them, for the name carried within it the character of the animal and its function. So one of our first tasks was to give assignments to all the other creatures and establish their life, space, and activity upon Earth. We were given the responsibility for the structure and functioning of the rest of life here.

The Two Trees

In the story of Eden, God placed two trees in the middle of the garden: the tree of life and the tree of the knowledge of good and evil (Genesis 2:9). He pointed out these trees and warned the humans not to eat the fruit of the tree of the knowledge of good and evil, stating that doing so would result in death (Genesis 2:16–17). Many people think this means that God placed a deliberate temptation in the garden to test the humans, and then He punished them with death for disobeying Him. I would like to offer a different and, I believe, more accurate explanation.

Adam and Eve were created in God's image, out of His heart of love and a desire to have intimate relationship with His human family. Being in His image meant that humans were given free and independent wills to do what they chose. This freedom of will is a love gift from God, who knows that real love is only love when it can be given or withheld at the choice of the lover. Had we been created with a built-in compulsion to love God, we would be less than His image, and our loving behavior would not be authentic love.

The two trees exist in the Eden story because they represent the essential dilemma of our free will. Not only are we given the power and authority to rule Earth, but we are also given the choice to rule it from a loving partnership with God or from an independent and rebellious defiance. The tree of life represented everything good, that is, everything that would be beneficial in its effects on us. In the tree of life God was offering us all the resources of wisdom, creativity, love, and joy that He possesses. He was opening the way for a positive partnership with Him. This way of living would allow us to pursue our abilities and uniqueness in an extended loving and supportive human community dwelling in a perfect world. The opportunities for exploration, learning, artistic expression of all types, and increase in responsibility in rulership would be unlimited.

The tree of the knowledge of good and evil represented the option to separate ourselves from God and go our own way. We would be limited to our physical capabilities and human knowledge without God's input, because we would be choosing to shut Him out. Note this tree contained the knowledge of both good and evil. In contrast to good, which is everything beneficial for us, evil denotes what is destructive, injurious, useless, and malignant. Since Adam and Eve already knew good, this knowledge introduced evil or calamity and then commingled it with good in a way that God knew would be impossible for humans to separate successfully. He knew that on our own and apart from His Spirit of divine wisdom, we would get bogged down in an endless swamp of dualistic thinking, never able to arrive at certainty about anything. We would be riddled by doubts, confusion, and continual attempts to judge our actions, resulting in clashing cycles of condemnation and justification of others and ourselves.

God knew the sense of futility and failure we would experience as we tried to keep figuring things out from our own limited self-centeredness. We would not have a large enough perspective to contain and process His reality. As a consequence, we would begin to lose our ability to understand responsibly the complexities of our world and effectively rule it. As we made increasingly inferior choices, trapped in the smallness of our human ability alone, we would lose touch with our original perfection and become increasingly frustrated and destructive in our behavior. He knew the tree of the knowledge of good and evil contained all this poison, and He warned us that it would harm us. He also knew that since we had dominion over the earth, the fruit of the tree of the knowledge of good and evil operating through us would radiate out, like the earthquake epicenter, and harm everything around us.

⑶

PARADISE LOST

The Bible doesn't tell us how long Adam and Eve lived in their Eden paradise. There is some hint that they had a routine, for God would walk and visit with them in the cool of the day (Genesis 3:8). The entire tragic drama that led to the loss of paradise and set human beings on a very different course from what God originally intended is contained in Genesis chapter 3.

Before the tragedy occurred, we are told, "The man and his

wife were both naked and were not embarrassed or ashamed in each other's presence" (Genesis 2:25, AMP). Although they may have been physically nude, this description tells us something profound about their relationship. There was so much love and trust between them that they had nothing to hide from each other. They knew that they could fully trust each other for support, encouragement, and complete acceptance. Can you imagine feeling completely comfortable revealing your entire self to anyone? Can you picture having confident trust that someone, anyone, loves you that unconditionally? It is difficult for us to imagine the security and peace in which Adam and Eve lived.

The Deception

Unfortunately they were not alone in the garden. Lucifer, who was their adversary and had an agenda to destroy them, was also present. Remember, he is a creature of stealth and deceit. The only thing you can know for sure about Lucifer is that he is totally untrustworthy. The Bible describes Lucifer as subtle or cunning and crafty (Genesis 3:1). When you read Genesis chapter 3, please be aware that the serpent that is mentioned is Lucifer. He approaches the pair and immediately begins to question what God has told them and what God's true motives are. He plants doubts about God's intentions, suggesting to them that if they eat the fruit of the tree of the knowledge of good and evil, something good, not evil, will happen. They will become like God. The eyes of their understanding will be open, and they will know good and evil.

A major problem with Lucifer is that he tells the blackest type of lie, combining truth and error. It was true they would have an understanding they did not currently possess, but it would be an understanding of good and evil mixed together, a reduced understanding based on their limited human intelligence and under the influence of their five physical senses. They would no longer be able to tap into the wisdom and creativity of God through His Spirit of life. They would completely lose touch with the dimension of spirit reality and the power and authority they had there. This would not make them more like God but less so. They were already in God's image and had been given dominion over the earth and the invitation to grow into rulership in the heavens as well. Without the ability to see into and know things in the spirit dimension of reality, they would be limited to what they could experience and learn through their physical senses. This would greatly reduce their dominion and authority and make life much more difficult in ways they could not imagine.

So Lucifer deceived them into thinking they would get more when in reality he was offering them less than they already had! Deception always works this way. It looks like something it is not, and too often you don't realize it until it's too late. You get stuck with something inferior or phony and realize you've been used or duped. Someone once said, "The grass always looks greener on the other side of a situation, until you get there and find it's just artificial turf." This is exactly what happened to Adam and Eve.

The Cover-up

Thinking they could become something greater on their own without God, they rebelled and ate the fruit of the tree of the knowledge of good and evil. But the outcome was not what Lucifer suggested it would be. Instead of having more and feeling good, they were immediately aware of their shame and vulnerability. They knew they had made a mistake and felt the sense of failure. They sensed their separateness from God and their loss of connection to His Spirit of life. The world looked and felt very different now, for they no longer were in touch with the spirit dimension of reality, only the physical dimension. Before their eyes the world was transforming into a dimension of reality they scarcely recognized.

For the first time in their lives, they experienced a hideous feeling: fear. It was a hollow, aching sensation that grabbed and twisted their guts, and they wanted to escape it and find security and peace again. So they ran and hid. But the terrible fear feeling just twisted and grew stronger, making their hearts pound and their minds race with all kinds of doubts and mistrust they had never experienced before. They were afraid to face God with their failure. They no longer even trusted one another. They each felt the need to "cover themselves." The story in Genesis describes them as covering themselves with fig leaves because they knew they were naked. Actually, they were each creating a "cover story" to excuse their rebellion.

When God came walking in the cool of the day, they were nowhere to be found. He asked where they were. They admitted to their error, but instead of coming to God seeking forgiveness and reconnection, they justified their behavior by blaming each other. They no longer trusted or were transparent with one another. Not only were they separated from God, but they were also separated from each other as well. Fearful and alone, they were now striving against one another. Does this sound familiar? How often have you been caught in a cycle of blame shifting with someone else, each of you convinced that your way of looking at the situation was correct, and excused your behavior? Although we've all done it, blame shifting never solves anything. Without resolution these cycles can escalate into hatred, resulting in all types of abuse, violence, prejudice, and, in the extreme, murder. Unresolved blame shifting among nations can even lead to wars.

The Exile

Residence in Eden was the result of living in harmony with God in the spirit dimension, but Adam and Eve had "fallen" from that dimension into the purely physical dimension. It was impossible for them to remain in Eden now in their limited physical human state. Not only was their residence in Eden affected, but also their ability to rule and have authority on Earth was diminished as well, for their dominion was not seated in their physical being but in their spiritual being. God intended that through willing partnership, the life of His Spirit would flow into their spirits to their physical bodies and to all the physical world around them. Adam and Eve in effect were to be "gods" and exercise their dominion by releasing this flow to bring and sustain life, health, peace, and abundance to the entire earth.

Severing their connection to God's Spirit of life cut them off from the power of His never-ending life. Additionally, they had unleashed the knowledge of evil into their world and would now have to cope with its constant influence. God told them what would now happen because of these tragic changes. The earth would no longer offer its abundance without effort to them. They would have to toil to make the earth produce their food. They would bear children in pain and sorrow. This was not just the physical pain of childbirth, but it was also the painful fear of knowing they would not be able to completely protect their children from evil and hurt in the world. They would continue to struggle against one another and experience times of alienation, even when they wanted to trust and be intimate with each other. Finally, in time, the evil now present in and around them would weaken and decay their physical bodies, and they would die. It was a disaster of cosmic proportions affecting all life on Earth permanently. It was the most profound loss humanity has ever suffered, and it changed everything about life as they knew it.

Our Present World: Are We in the Matrix?

In the movie *The Matrix*, Thomas Anderson (Keanu Reeves) is a computer hacker who pirates computer programs for profit on his own time and, by day, works as a computer programmer in a large firm. As the movie opens, he receives a strange message from another dimension through his computer. By following a series of prompts he enters the surrealistic-appearing world of the resistance fighters. There he discovers that his world, which appeared so normal and predictable, is actually the Matrix, "a computer-generated dreamworld built to keep humans under control." The Matrix is run by machine beings originally created by humans as AI (artificial intelligence) machines. The machines have become self-generating but still need the thermal and electromagnetic energy given off by humans to run themselves. They manipulate humans through the deceptive virtual reality of the Matrix and use them as living batteries or energy sources.

Thomas, or "Neo" (his computer alias), meets Morpheus, a pioneer in the resistance. The resistance fighters are those humans who have somehow "unplugged" and broken out of the deception of the Matrix. They enter the Matrix undercover to subvert the control of the machines. They are also carrying on warfare with the machines in the "real" world, those parts of Earth not controlled by the Matrix. Most of them live in Zion, the city of freedom, close to the center of the earth.

Morpheus explains the Matrix to Neo this way: "The Matrix is everywhere.... You can see it when you look out your window or when you turn on your television. You can feel it when you go to work, when you go to church, when you pay your taxes. It is the world that has been pulled over your eyes to blind you from the truth...that you are a slave, Neo. Like everyone else you were born into...a prison that you cannot taste or see or touch—a prison for your mind....No one can be told what the Matrix is...you have to see it for yourself.

"You're here because you know something. What you know you can't explain, but you feel it. You've felt it your entire life, that there's something wrong with the world."[1]

Later, Morpheus takes Neo on a practice walk through a computer simulation of the Matrix. As they are walking down what appears to be an ordinary big-city street, Morpheus comments, "As long as the Matrix exists, human beings will never be free.[2] ...Most of these people are not ready to be unplugged.

And many of them are so inured, so hopelessly dependent on the system, that they will fight to protect it."[3] When Neo meets the Oracle, a person of wisdom who has been around since the beginning of the resistance, she informs him: "There are programs running all over the place. The ones doing their job, doing what they were meant to do, are invisible. You'd never even know they were here."[4]

Morpheus shows Neo a television screen with city scenes. He tells Neo, "This is the world that you know....It exists now only as part of a neural-interactive simulation that we call the Matrix. You've been living in a dreamworld, Neo."[5] The screen dramatically changes and looks like the rubble and carnage left over from a possible nuclear attack. As Neo pulls back in horror, Morpheus continues, "This is the world as it exists today. Welcome to the desert of the real...."[6] At this point the shock is so great for Neo that he passes out.

You may agree that a computer-simulated deception on a mass scale may make for a fascinating sci-fi flick, but it's hardly anything that could ever become a reality. I agree that we don't need to lose sleep about being taken over by plotting AI machines. But I would like you to consider the possibility that we may be living in massive deception from another source, a spiritual one. When Adam and Eve first left Eden, they could probably remember many things about it, including some memories of what living in the spiritual dimension was like. Undoubtedly they passed stories on to their children and grandchildren about the wonders of Eden and the incredible authority and creativity they enjoyed in partnership with God's Spirit of life. However, their day-to-day reality was one of physical hardship and the type of learning experiences their physical senses could provide. Firsthand experience with the broader spiritual reality became dimmer as it faded into the past. With successive generations, it was largely forgotten or relegated to isolated experiences of a religious or superstitious nature. Dependence on the sense-based physical dimension became dominant.

We humans became very good at establishing highly structured ways to use our five senses to explore and investigate the world around us to help us explain, predict, and, in some cases, control natural events. These discoveries often benefited our lives in laborsaving or knowledge-enhancing technology, resulting in better ways to raise crops and fight disease and in faster ways to communicate and travel. But our journey into knowledge has been mixed. In an increasingly intensive spiral of seeking and questing for more and more knowledge, we opened up an unending chain of Pandora's boxes, each inviting us into deeper mysteries of knowledge. It doesn't matter if it's done in the name of science, art, literature, economics, or environmental protection; we now have the world so highly fragmented and specialized that it has become impossible to integrate what we "know"! It's as if we have been swallowed alive by the tree of knowledge. Yet our thirst for still more knowledge appears insatiable.

We seem to believe that more knowledge will help us to eventually solve everything. But even with all our accumulated knowledge, we still fight and war incessantly. We pollute and poison our world and ourselves in the name of technological progress. We slash, burn, and poison our bodies in the name of medical care, sometimes to such an extreme that we make the leechings of a few centuries ago look beneficent by comparison.

We continuously find that our knowledge, which we hoped would solve certain issues, only creates more issues by opening new areas of dispute and debate. And for all our efforts, our dominion of Earth continues to elude us. We have not regained what we lost in the garden.

The Spiritual Matrix

Why do we struggle so when we are obviously bright, creative, inventive, and motivated creatures? I believe our problem lies in the spiritual dimension of reality from which we became separated. While our awareness of that dimension dimmed and was replaced by our preoccupation with the physical dimension, spiritual reality did not weaken or go away. We simply lost touch with it, but it continues to exert its influence on us. Just like with the Matrix, we may not be able to detect it with our smell, touch, sight, or taste, but it is still present. And it is an active place populated by beings, some like angels who are helpful, but also some like Lucifer and his renegade angels (also called demons) who want to destroy us.

We did not lose our legal right to dominion when we fell out of the spirit dimension, but we became seriously limited in our ability to understand what was going on around us. We became blind to what was happening spiritually. Think of it as trying to function without your eyesight. You still can, of course, but you have some significant limitations. Lucifer, our adversary, was quick to use these limitations to his advantage. Knowing our spiritual darkness, he began to weave a web of deception by using our human reasoning and feelings against us.

Separated from God's Spirit of life, we are no match for Lucifer. He is highly intelligent and can think rings around us, commingling truth and error in such complex ways that it would take multiple lifetimes to sort out. He has been around for thousands of years observing us, and he knows all the most effective ways to instill fear in us. He can stir up our anger, jealousy, and strife; he can ignite insatiable passion in us for almost anything and everything. He has never stopped his Eden tactic of tempting us with trinkets like fame, money, and power in exchange for our bartering away our godlike integrity, honesty, authority, and dominion. Although he cannot directly seize our dominion, he can and does seduce us into relinquishing it.

His primary strategies are stealth and deception. Like the invisible programs always running in *The Matrix*, Satan prefers to operate undetected. He likes to lull us into believing he doesn't exist and that we are truly independent and in control. We become more and more complacent as we sink into his delusional spiritual matrix of convenience, compromise, and comfort. We have no idea that we are in a prison of deception, already deep in bondage as our minds become progressively more blind and oblivious to his manipulations. We are plugged into his spiritual matrix, and often without our knowing it, our actions dance to his strings.

The Bible describes the reality of this spiritual matrix and clearly identifies Satan as the mastermind behind it:

> For the god of this world *[Satan]* has blinded the unbelievers' minds [that they should not discern the truth].
> —2 Corinthians 4:4, AMP

We know [positively]...the whole world [around us] is under the power of the evil one.

—1 John 5:19, AMP

There are numerous instances where the Bible describes Satan's character as both dishonest and destructive:

He [Satan] was a murderer from the beginning and does not stand in the truth, because there is no truth in him. When he speaks falsehood, he speaks what is natural to him, for he is a liar [himself], and the father of lies and of all that is false.

—John 8:44, AMP

And it is no wonder, for Satan himself masquerades as an angel of light.

—2 Corinthians 11:14, AMP

The thief [Satan] comes only to steal and kill and destroy.

—John 10:10

The Bible warns that consistently giving in to destructive emotions and uncontrolled passions can open us up to deeper bondage with Satan. For example, it warns that people who are angry and engage in frequent quarreling need to "come to their senses and escape from the trap of the devil, who has taken them captive to do his will" (2 Timothy 2:26). And people who do not control their passions are described as having "the mind of the flesh [which is sense and reason without the Holy Spirit]" (Romans 8:6, AMP). This verse goes on to say that the mind of the flesh "is death [the death that comprises all the miseries arising from sin, both here and hereafter]."

The Bible is very clear that due to the Fall, we are all under the influence of this spiritual matrix. We cannot free ourselves on our own. Our adversary is too experienced and too merciless to allow anyone his or her freedom. No one knowingly wants to be the puppet of someone else. We were not created to be the slaves of a fallen angel and do his bidding, but we were created to have dominion over him and subdue him! Fortunately, although we separated ourselves from God's Spirit of life, He never separated His love from us. In the most daring undercover operation of all time, He executed a plan to free us from bondage and return the integrity of our dominion, while leaving our free will intact. We will look at this undercover operation in chapter 5.

⊲(4)⊳

ALIEN BATTLE LINES

Before television, back in the days of radio, dramas were produced using dialogue and sound effects. Listeners had to use their imaginations to supply the visual effects. In October 30, 1938, a very famous incident occurred in which, to put it mildly, a large number of Americans allowed their imaginations to run away with them. Actor Orson Welles decided to produce a radio drama about a Martian alien invasion of the earth. It was an adaptation of the H. G. Wells's science-fiction novel *War of the Worlds*.[1] It was presented as a newscast that got interrupted, at first by unusual sightings, and then by actual aliens entering the city and the broadcast booth. It was produced with dramatic dialogue and increasingly chaotic sound effects. It was done very well, but with one major problem. No one announced beforehand that it was a drama, and millions of Americans thought they were listening to an actual newscast that had been interrupted by an alien invasion. Some listeners actually became hysterical! I believe the incident resulted in some broadcasting codes being enacted to prevent that type of error from occurring again!

The incident illustrates an important point. Most of us believe that an alien invasion would involve some type of huge catastrophe for life on Earth. A recent example is the movie *Independence Day*, in which aliens begin destroying major world population centers. Or if done undercover, an invasion would turn disastrous as aliens take over the bodies of humans and then begin attacking us. (Think of the films *Alien* and *Invasion of the Body Snatchers*.) It's harder to imagine an undercover war of the worlds executed to benefit us and waged so effectively that we were virtually unaware of its occurrence. But I want you to know that this is exactly what happened here on Earth two thousand years ago, and we are still feeling its effects. Let me explain.

The Dilemma

In the last chapter we discussed the fall of Adam and Eve and the disastrous consequences that followed, not only for them and for us as their descendants, but also for all other life on Earth as well. Decay, disease, and disorder invaded every aspect of plant, animal, and environmental functioning. One of the most serious consequences for us was that we literally fell out of the spirit dimension and were reduced to the physical dimension. From our new limited perspective, it was impossible to know what was going on in the spirit dimension, and we became easy prey for the deceptive manipulations of our arch adversary, Satan. Much like the unsuspecting humans trapped in the movie *The Matrix,* we are also in bondage. We are in a prison, a "spiritual matrix" we cannot readily detect. We are under the influence of a merciless fallen angel who frequently dupes us for his purposes.

Though we rebelled in the Fall and chose to separate ourselves from God and His resources, He never stopped loving us and desiring to reconnect with us. But now there were some major hindrances that had not existed before. In order to understand what these hindrances were, we need to look at our common definitions of life and death. In the spirit dimension, these words have a deeper meaning than just the presence or absence of physical existence. In the Bible, life and God are synonymous. Life is what makes God, God. But it is not just an energy that animates and provides mobility and power. The life of God is life in an absolute sense. It is so total, so untouched by any weakness, decay, defect, or death in any way, so pure and perfect, that it is referred to as holiness. Nothing less than this absolute life can stand in the presence of God, or it will be evaporated by His purity and holiness. I think you can see that once Adam and Eve fell, they were no longer able to enter God's presence and communicate directly with Him as they had formerly. Their newly acquired acquaintance with evil effectively severed such contact.

Death is much more than the cessation of physical existence.

In its ultimate sense, it is separation from God, who is absolute life. Anything less than absolute life, less than perfection, is already touched by death. Separation from God allows the entrance of all forms of death, such as pain, suffering, disease, mental or emotional torment, hatred, envy, doubt, and fear, to name a few. Probably the most tragic outcome of this separation from God is spiritual death. This is the loss of access to the spirit dimension and God's resources like peace, health, power, authority, prosperity, and so on that flow from God's absolute life. While Adam and Eve did not physically die for some time, they did die spiritually the day they ate the fruit of the tree of the knowledge of good and evil, even as God had warned them:

> But you must not eat from the tree of the knowledge of good and evil, for when you eat of it you will surely die.
> —Genesis 2:17

Spiritually dead meant being completely cut off from the spirit dimension, which made it more difficult for humans to contact and communicate with God. Their ability to see and understand anything spiritual was virtually nil. Additionally, under the constant influence of evil, humans were trapped in the delusions of Satan's spiritual matrix. They were thrown into confusion, chaos, doubt, mistrust, and fear as a principle called sin invaded them.

Sin is the result of choosing rebellion against God; it always leads to evil, trouble, misfortune, sorrow, wrongdoing, and every type of offense you can think of. It is so much more than bad actions. It is a perversion of absolute life itself. It is the twisting of truth into error, giving way to a lifestyle of mediocrity and compromise. This lifestyle falls far short of the mark of God's absolute life. Sin is like a flesh-eating virus that invades the will and begins to poison and pollute it. In the end, we can even want to do something honorable and noble, yet trip ourselves up in the attempt, leaving us with a frustrated sense of failure. If you've ever made a resolution to change something about yourself and failed (who hasn't?), then you know what I am talking about. We end up being angry and disappointed with ourselves and feeling more than a little hopeless.

Inherent in the fruit of the tree of the knowledge of good and evil was the virus of sin. The Bible tells us, "The wages of sin is death" (Romans 6:23). So sin brings both spiritual and physical death and all the other forms that evil can take. Somehow God had to find a way to work around these obstacles and make it possible to reconnect with us. But He would not violate how He created us, in His image. He would respect our free will and right to choose. He would not deceive or manipulate us. He would honor our dominion of Earth. He would not forcibly take control or trick us into relinquishing our dominion. He loves us so much that He wants to preserve who we choose to be, even if we choose to continue in our separation from Him.

Our free will and our legal right of dominion are the biggest wild cards in our situation, for only we can determine what we will do with them. Satan will do his best to pressure and influence our decisions. God will honor our choices. Ultimately we hold the final say for ourselves and the earth, our domain.

The Promise

God knew that the moment Adam and Eve fell, they lost entrance into the spirit realm. He wanted to give them a concrete physical sign that, although they would no longer be able to walk into His presence, He nonetheless was still near. He had not abandoned them. He did this in two related ways. First He announced to the serpent, Lucifer, "I will put enmity between you and the woman, and between your offspring and hers; he will crush your head, and you will strike his heel" (Genesis 3:15). Here God was clearly indicating to Lucifer that although he had won an important battle in Eden, the war was far from over. In the end, a human would defeat him. To Adam and Eve, this meant that the tragic situation that had just occurred was not permanent. A champion, a deliverer, would come one day and reverse the curse into which they had fallen.

Next, God does something that demonstrates His heart of love to Adam and Eve. He kills an animal and makes a garment out of its skin and clothes them. In one sense, this is a practical act of love. God knows that the earth outside the garden will not be climate controlled. They will need more than fig leaves to keep them warm. But the act has a far more significant meaning. Remember that Adam and Eve covered themselves with fig leaves after the Fall to hide their nakedness or, put another way, to cloak their sin. They then devised a "cover story" by blaming one another to justify their rebellious act. Their blame shifting did nothing to free them from the virus of sin that had begun to engulf them. If anything, as an act of dishonesty, the blame shifting just mired them deeper in the sin.

But God's action offered them a true covering, a true cleansing from the sin. Sin always results in death. By sacrificing an animal and covering Adam and Eve with its bloody skin, God was imparting life for their sin by shedding the life force, the blood, of another living being. In this way He modeled for them that they could cover over their sin and release themselves from it through sacrifices. The blood offering would constantly remind them of the seriousness of sin, which not only leads to physical death that they could clearly see in the sacrifice, but also results in spiritual death, which is separation from God.

The only thing powerful enough to swallow up death and neutralize it is life, but not the physical life of an animal, only the absolute life of God. Every animal sacrifice was a concrete reminder to them of this reality. Animal sacrifices had to be repeated because, while they could cleanse from sin, they could not destroy its power. So sin continued, and people continued to need cleansing. But in a way they could not possibly understand, the practice of animal sacrifice was also a picture pointing to something far more powerful. It was a foreshadowing of the ultimate exchange to come. God's absolute life would be offered to destroy forever the power of sin and death over humans and all other life on Earth.

Most of the Old Testament contains stories about how God continued to interact with various individuals. He wanted them to understand He was still present and what type of a being He is. Since their direct accessibility into God's presence in the spirit dimension was no longer available, God had to get creative in communicating to them in ways they could understand. He had to deal with them through the physical realm, mentally, and through events, because spiritually they were in darkness. Over and over He reminded them of His promise that one day they would have the opportunity to be set free from sin and death and enter the spirit dimension again. Let's look briefly at two different ways that God communicated His promise to them. One was through an event, a literal physical deliverance, and the other was verbally through prophecy.

Deliverance Through Death

If you have Jewish friends, ask them what Passover is, and they will be able to tell you this story. Thousands of years ago the children of Israel were slaves in Egypt. They longed to be free, but after four hundred years of bondage, most of them had probably given up hope. But God had not forgotten them. He used an Israelite baby named Moses, who was actually adopted and raised by Pharaoh's daughter, to be His spokesperson to set them free. The details of this incredible story are in the first fourteen chapters of Exodus, the second book in the Bible.

When Moses approached him and asked that the Israelites go free, Pharaoh was reluctant to simply open the exit gates and bid them farewell. Having a large, basically free labor force was a tremendous economic advantage, so he absolutely refused to consider their release. What happens next is a fascinating story as a series of calamities struck Egypt while Pharaoh continued to refuse to release the Israelites. With every request for release and every refusal by Pharaoh, the calamities became more severe. Finally, all Pharaoh's advisors counseled him to relent and let the Israelites go free, but he stubbornly refused. The final calamity was death to all the firstborn children in Egypt. Although warned by God through Moses, Pharaoh still refused to release the children of Israel.

God instructed Moses to tell the Israelites that they must take a healthy lamb and kill it. They were to take the lamb's blood and put it on the sides and top of their front doors and then roast the lamb and eat it. They were to stay up all night, fully dressed and packed, ready to leave Egypt. God informed them that a death angel would come through Egypt. Whenever it saw a doorway covered with blood, it would pass over that house and not go in. But wherever it did not see the blood, it would enter in and take the life of the firstborn in that house. Because they heard and obeyed God, the Israelites lost no people to death, but all the Egyptians had a death in their houses. Pharaoh quickly called for Moses and told him to take the Israelites and leave immediately!

To this day Jewish people all over the world celebrate this event, which they call Passover, for the death angel passed over them and God set them free. It's an incredible story of God's love and protection for the Jewish people at that time. But it is also a picture for all humans of God's desire to reconnect with us. In effect, God is telling us: "Even though you are in bondage to sin and death, stuck in the spiritual matrix, I am going to deliver you, just as I did with the Jews in Egypt. I am going to provide a way, the blood of a perfect Lamb that will set you free from the death angel and from the power of sin." The story event becomes a powerful picture reminder of God's promise to us that the curse will be reversed. He will offer us the freedom to return to the spirit dimension and regain everything we lost in the Fall. Many other Old Testament stories show us how God uses different events in history to remind us that He is still present and has not forgotten His promise.

Prophetic Intentions

I hope you remember from chapter 1 that the Bible is a book with many prophecies, about twenty-five hundred, and nearly two thousand of those have been fulfilled. I'd like to quote two of them here for you to consider. One tells us God's ultimate intention, and the other reveals part of His plan for achieving that intention. In Isaiah 14:24–27 we find:

The LORD Almighty has sworn,

> "Surely, as I have planned, so it will be,
>   and as I have purposed, so it will stand.
> I will crush the Assyrian in my land;
>   on my mountains I will trample him down.
> His yoke will be taken from my people,
>   and his burden removed from their shoulders."

> This is the plan determined for the whole world;
>   this is the hand stretched out over all the nations.
> For the LORD Almighty has purposed, and who can
>   thwart him?
>   His hand is stretched out, and who can turn it back?

At the time it was given, this prophecy referred to a dire political situation in which God promised to deliver Israel from oppressing enemies. But the statement is much broader than this historic event, for God goes on to say that this is His intention for the whole world and for all the nations. He intends to crush the oppressor and remove the yoke of bondage from His people everywhere. God is again reminding us that He intends to set us free and reverse the curse that holds us captive. Over and over He repeats this theme to us in the Old Testament. He wants us to believe Him and be confident. He wants us to trust in His love for us. He is present and has a plan.

In other prophecies God begins to reveal the particulars of His plan to us. In Isaiah 7:14 He says, "Therefore the Lord himself will give you a sign: The virgin will be with child and give birth to a son, and will call him Immanuel [God with us]." Isaiah 9:6–7 provides further details: "For to us a child is born, to us a son is given, and the government will be upon his shoulders. And he will be called Wonderful Counselor, Mighty God, Everlasting Father, Prince of Peace. Of the increase of his government and peace there will be no end." These are references to the arrival of a special person, someone very much like God Himself. This person is the central figure in God's undercover operation to reverse the curse and restore us to our originally created dominion.

⟨ 5 ⟩

THE SUPREME
UNDERCOVER OPERATION

In preparation for launching His undercover plan, God wanted to communicate to humans that true good, that is, pure good that is not mixed with evil, still existed. The results of the Fall were so deep and so dark that humans had lost touch with the goodness they were created to enjoy. They had no idea how far they had fallen and how compromised their understanding of good had become. He wanted to keep alive in them a spark of the original place they occupied in the spirit dimension. He did not want them to lose sight altogether of who they were created to be. He wanted to help them remember, so He gave them the Ten Commandments. The first four commandments refer to our relationship to God, and the last six refer to our relationship with one another. Together they describe what perfect goodness looks like in these relationships. You can find all ten commandments listed in Exodus 20:1–17.

God knew that in their fallen condition, humans would not be able to perfectly follow these laws. But He wanted to help them remember that they were originally created to be in His image. He wanted to give them some idea about what living in His image would look like. He told them to constantly focus on the Law and follow it. Doing so would keep the memory of life, absolute life in Eden, before them, even if they could not attain it. They would have difficulties and experience failure, but they could sacrifice and obtain release from their sin. But they would continue to remember something about how their life had originally been. This would help them hold on to the hope of its return.

We have previously discussed that God promised humans that the curse would be reversed. He was not willing to violate people's will, their free choice, for this would make them less than created in His image. But He knew that humans were trapped in a spiritual matrix, in darkness, unable even to see the prison they were in. It was impossible to communicate with them in the spirit dimension. Through their deception, they had handed over much of their dominion to Satan. How could God make contact with them and communicate who He was, what He was like, or what His intentions were? Like the challenge of the resistance fighters in the movie *The Matrix*, God's challenge was how to set up an undercover operation within the spiritual matrix itself. It must be an undercover operation that would go undetected and be able to destroy Satan's spiritual matrix from within. So the operation must be executed by a human being, for only a human being had the legal right to exercise free will in the dominion of the earth. If God seized control, He would diminish an essential element that He created in humans—their free will.

The Plan

So God devised an incredible plan totally outside our ability to comprehend it. He would go undercover and become a human being. In this way He would gain access to humanity imprisoned in Satan's spiritual matrix. But this would not be a typical undercover operation in which someone disguises him or herself and penetrates behind enemy lines. It was the supreme undercover maneuver. God did not cloak Himself with humanity. He was not coming as God in a human disguise. In an incredible act of love, He laid aside all His privileges as deity and became a true human being, a person we know as Jesus of Nazareth. He became unequal with God, not by giving up His divinity, but by taking on humanity. The Bible describes it this way:

> *[Jesus]*...being essentially one with God and in the form of God [possessing the fullness of the attributes which make God God], did not think this equality with God was something to be eagerly grasped or retained, but stripped Himself [of all privileges and rightful dignity], so as to

assume the guise of a servant (slave), in that He became like men and was born a human being.

—Philippians 2:6–7, AMP

This event was so significant that it is completely unparalleled by anything else in all history! The divine ET was once again extending an invitation to humankind. By becoming one of them, He was opening the opportunity to directly communicate and connect once again. The heavens (His dwelling place in the spirit dimension) were literally bursting with anticipation and joy, so much so that a group of angels appeared to some shepherds tending sheep on a hillside outside Bethlehem, the birthplace of Jesus. The angels were surrounded by bright light and were exuberantly singing praise to God and giving this message to the shepherds: "Peace on earth, goodwill from God to men." They were literally announcing, "Wholeness, restoration to the earth. God is pouring out His goodness to humans. He has come to heal the breach caused by the Fall." They were making it clear that God was about to fulfill His promise to reverse the curse.

The event I just described may have a familiar feel to you. It should, because this is the Christmas story. For two thousand years it has been celebrated to commemorate God becoming one of us and keeping His promise to deliver us. His gift, utterly relinquishing His rights as God to share our human existence with us, is so staggering that to this day we celebrate it by giving gifts to one another. It is a special day, a day we remember how the spiritual and physical dimensions intersected in a moment of eternal cosmic significance for our benefit.

Jesus entered the earth the way every other human does, by

being prenatally formed in the uterus of His mother and by being born as a helpless and totally dependent baby. However, there is one distinguishing feature of His conception and birth. Jesus was conceived by a virgin, for God Himself is His Father. In this way He entered Earth fully human, but a human without the virus of sin. A human fully connected to the spirit dimension. A human like Adam before the Fall. Like Adam, Jesus had to continually choose between the Spirit of God's absolute life and going His own way by preferring the knowledge of good and evil.

The influence of evil and the principle of sin were constantly pressuring Him just as they do every human in the matrix. But He consistently chose God's Spirit of life and stayed connected to the spirit dimension. He did not yield to temptation and sin. Hebrews 4:15 states that Jesus was able to understand and share our feelings about weakness and vulnerability to the influence of temptation. He was tempted in every way that we are, but He did not sin. This description makes it clear that He did not have some magic protection against sin and evil as God. He was still God, but God limiting Himself to being a real human being. As a human being He had to make active choices to stay connected to the spirit dimension by saying yes to God's Spirit of life and no to all temptation to go His own way. Jesus was freely choosing to live the life that God had originally intended and hoped Adam and Eve would choose to live.

Take a moment and reflect on what this means. The divine ET, the being who set the universe in motion, decided to enter the physical dimension as one of us, a human being. He was born, nursed at His mother's breasts, and had to learn to walk, speak, and read like any other child. He attended synagogue and memorized the Law, or Torah, and had a bar mitzvah, like any other Jewish boy. He played childhood games with peers and learned the skills of being a carpenter by working with His adoptive father, Joseph. He was living a completely ordinary human life in Nazareth, a small, nondescript village, well removed from the cultural and religious centers of his day. And this routine existence continued until He was roughly thirty years old. Can you imagine an undercover operation literally incubating for thirty years before being implemented? But God was patient, and He intended to get the full imprint of being human firsthand. The whole time Jesus was daily learning how to choose the Spirit of life and how to walk in trust and obedience to God, His Father. These would be very important lessons for successful completion of His mission on Earth.

Mission Launch

Do you ever wonder what God looks like? Jesus said, "Anyone who has seen me has seen the Father [God]" (John 14:9). He did not mean, "I physically look like the Father." He meant, "Watch what I do, what kind of a person I am, and you will see the character of the Father." Jesus made it very clear that He was following the example of His Father, God. He stated, "I tell you the truth, the Son can do nothing by himself; he can do only what he sees his Father doing, because whatever the Father does the Son also does" (John 5:19). Another time He said, "I do nothing on my own but speak just what the Father has taught me" (John 8:28).

Fortunately for us, Jesus "went public" at about thirty years of age. An important part of His mission was to help us understand who God is and to remind us of who we are. He spent the next three years demonstrating what God was really like, as well as showing us what we were originally intended to be. We needed to see this in order to fully grasp what God was inviting us back into. We needed to know we could trust and rely on Him to be true to His Word to us. Jesus accomplished this by what He said, how He lived, and how He treated others. Looking at a sample of His life will help us to better understand His mission and the nature of the Father God's heart. Again, fortunately for us, some details of His words and actions were recorded by His followers in Matthew, Mark, Luke, and John, the first four books in the New Testament. These books are frequently referred to as the Gospels.

Radical Transformation

When you read the Gospels, you will notice that Jesus's favorite topic of conversation was what He called "the kingdom of heaven," or "the kingdom of God." For Jesus, these terms refer to life in the spirit dimension or living in connection with God's Spirit of life. It is the sphere of God's rule where we originally partnered with Him in reigning. From this spirit dimension, we were to use God's resources and exercise the power and authority He gave us in order to have dominion over the physical dimension here on the earth. Jesus was constantly telling people that the kingdom of heaven is near, close by, or at hand. (See Matthew 4:17; Matthew 10:7; Luke 10:9.) He wanted them to understand that God's sphere of rule, the spirit dimension, is all around them. It is close to them, and the way back into it is being opened up.

He was here to announce that God wants to reinstate humans to their original place of power and authority and partnership with Him. In Luke 12:32, Jesus assured the people who were listening to and following Him. He said, "Do not be seized with alarm and struck with fear, little flock, for it is your Father's good pleasure to give you the kingdom!" (AMP). In one instance the people in a certain village wanted Jesus to stay on with them longer. So they tried to prevent Him from leaving. He told them, "I must preach the good news of the kingdom of God to the other towns also, because that is why I was sent" (Luke 4:43).

The Fall set in motion a radical transformation that took us out of living in the spirit dimension and limited us to living in the physical dimension. Jesus makes it clear that another radical transformation must occur in us before we can "see" or be aware of the kingdom of God. This is because the kingdom of God is not part of the physical dimension where it can register on our physical senses. It is from the spirit dimension and has to be perceived through the eyes of our human spirit. But our human spirit can do this only when it is reconnected to God's Spirit of life. It is not something we can accomplish on our own.

You cannot think your way into the kingdom of God, nor can you meditate yourself into that dimension. A lifetime devoted to theological study will not open the door. Consulting with mediums, familiar spirits, tarot cards, crystal balls, the stars, tea leaves, or palm readers will not tell you anything about the kingdom of God or get you one step closer to it. Achieving altered states of consciousness through various physical disciplines, martial arts, or use of drugs may indeed open you up to "other world" contacts programmed by Satan's spiritual matrix to deceive you. But they are dead ends, and they will not lead you into God's kingdom. Never forget that Lucifer (Satan) loves to masquerade as an angel of light, but his "enlightenment" is a fraud. It appears real, but it is designed only to snare, deceive, and manipulate you. Only God's Spirit of life can open His kingdom to you.

While we cannot enter the kingdom of God through our own efforts, we are not to be passive. Jesus indicates there are several actions required of us to set this radical transformation into operation. First and foremost, we must be willing to repent for rebelling against God and going our own way. This does not mean we beat ourselves up with guilt. It does mean we are willing to turn from the present way we think about life, others, and ourselves. We must be honest with ourselves and admit that we cannot solve or fix all our problems or the difficulties in the world around us. We need to acknowledge that we are tired of being frustrated, fearful, angry, and hurtful to others and ourselves. We have to own that we have tried many times to make things better in a variety of ways with mixed results. But we always end up dissatisfied, feeling there must be "something more" even if we don't know what it is. We must be willing to turn from all these previous efforts and failures and move in a new direction. We must embrace a whole new way of thinking that comes from the spirit dimension of God's kingdom.

We must be transformed in a way that is so basic, so profound, that Jesus described it as being "born again." In the movie *The Matrix*, after Neo accepts Morpheus's invitation to "see the real world," he goes through a major transformation that changes every part of his being. He gets "unplugged" from the Matrix and "cleansed" so he can "see" reality. He has to be debugged and deprogrammed so he can begin to "see" the delusions of the Matrix. And even after his transformation is complete, he still has to relearn who he is and how he will function in his new life outside the Matrix. This takes time, but as he progresses, he becomes more skilled and stronger.

Our transformation out of the deceptions of Satan's spiritual matrix and into the spirit dimension of the kingdom of God is a similar process. We must be cleansed and get unhooked from Satan's manipulations. We must be deprogrammed so we can see ourselves as God intended us to be. We must learn how to partner with Him and how to take back our rightful power and authority here on Earth. We must become "kingdom people."

Jesus described this process to a curious Jewish religious leader who came to Him with questions wanting to know more. (See John 3:1–21.) This leader listened to Jesus and saw His actions and knew that Jesus was connected to God. Jesus told him that unless he was "born again," he could not ever see or experience the kingdom of God. This puzzled the leader, for he was an adult. How could he possibly go back and be born again? Did Jesus mean that he was to have another birth, another life experience here on Earth? No, Jesus was not talking about any reincarnation process. He told the leader that what is born of the physical dimension is physical; what is born of the Spirit of God is spiritual. By this He meant that this leader needed to have a spiritual transformation. Jesus stated that trying to understand the spirit dimension from the physical dimension of the five senses is like trying to capture the wind. You can hear the sound of the wind, but you don't know where it comes from or where it goes. It is the same with understanding the spirit dimension. It is impossible to "see" what is going on in the spirit dimension without being transformed or "born again."

Reclaiming Our Identity

Not only does God want people to be transformed, but He also wants them to reclaim their identity. God calls humans back to their first identity as kingdom people. But just what do kingdom people look and act like? When Adam and Eve fell, they became less than what God originally intended them to be. Part of Jesus's mission was to help humans understand their true identity as God designed them. One way Jesus demonstrated this was by what He said to people and how He interacted with them. Jesus welcomed sincere seekers from every part of society. Who a person was and what type of social status they had were of no importance to Jesus. He was looking within at their motives and attitudes. He saw who they truly were beneath their social standing and outward behaviors.

If they were seeking the kingdom of God, He was open and available to them. He walked and talked with them; He answered their questions; and He ate, drank, and socialized with them. Some people who sought Him out were prostitutes and tax collectors; some were disabled people and lepers. Most of them were not highly educated. Very few were wealthy. Jesus accepted and spent time with all of them. He understood that people are often lonely and afraid, feeling empty inside and not knowing where to turn. He knew they were trapped in Satan's spiritual matrix and were in bondage, unhappy, and distressed. One time He looked at a crowd that had gathered and felt such compassion for them because He could see how uncertain and hurting they were. To His eyes of love, the people looked like sheep that had lost their shepherd. They were just wandering about lost and looking for their purpose.

Many people flocked to hear Jesus and were impressed with His words about the kingdom of God. But not everyone thought Jesus picked the right kind of people with whom to associate. Most of the religious leaders of His day referred to Jesus as a "party boy" and a drunkard. They prided themselves on living lives of moral purity and having nothing to do with anyone who was not socially respectable. They couldn't believe that Jesus chose to relate with such social pond scum, and they openly criticized Him for it. Jesus seldom had an angry or harsh word for anyone, but for the religious leaders He had plenty. He saw how arrogant they were. They thought they were better than the average person because they were highly educated and followed a rigid code of moral ethics. They thought they were keeping the commandments of God by doing this, but Jesus had a different opinion of them. The Law was supposed to help people under-stand the pure goodness of God's Spirit of life. But the religious leaders took the Law and turned it into a detailed list of dos and don'ts. They lost the Spirit of life, which was the goodness and heart of the Law. They turned it into a set of empty religious practices that didn't produce either life or goodness.

Jesus did not observe their list of dos and don'ts. In fact, He frequently violated their list, for He knew that the true spirit of the Law produced change in the attitudes of a person's heart. It was not the practice of religious acts. When the religious leaders harassed Jesus for "breaking the Law," He confronted them bluntly:

> Woe to you...pretenders (hypocrites)! For you shut the kingdom of heaven in men's faces; for you neither enter yourselves, nor do you allow those who are about to go in to do so.
>
> —Matthew 23:13, AMP

> Woe to you...pretenders (hypocrites)! For you are like tombs that have been whitewashed, which look beautiful on the outside but inside are full of dead men's bones and everything impure. Just so, you also outwardly seem to people to be just and upright but inside you are full of pretense and lawlessness and iniquity....You serpents! You spawn of vipers! How can you escape the penalty to be suffered in hell (Gehenna)?
>
> —Matthew 23:27–28, 33, AMP

In contrast to the behavior and judgmental attitudes of the religious leaders, Jesus modeled the true spirit of the Law. He taught people to love and respect one another and to treat each other with equality and fairness. He told people to be quick to forgive each other and slow to take offense and get angry. They were not to be doormats. They were to confront one another when they had difficulties and seek true reconciliation, rather than cut one another off or attempt to verbally or physically harm each other. Jesus knew that this was the only way that people would ever be able to climb out of the rut of endless strife, arguments, and wars that solve nothing and just destroy people and the environment. He knew that this type of relating would lead people back into wholeness, joy, and reconnection with God's Spirit of life. Jesus knew that to live this way would require a larger and more courageous heart. People could only acquire this type of heart by being transformed or born again. He taught them these and many other principles of kingdom living so they would understand their need for transformation. He wanted people to seek the kingdom of God and choose to be born again.

⤚(6)⤙

LOVE IS NOT
A FOUR-LETTER WORD

Jesus wanted people to actively seek transformation and choose to unplug from Satan's spiritual matrix. He knew this was the only way they could begin experiencing life in the kingdom of God. But to do this they would have to trust God completely. Unplugging from the matrix would mean turning away from the life they knew, and were used to, and embracing a new way of being and experiencing reality. In order to convince people to take such a radical step and want to reclaim their identity, Jesus had to show them that God was trustworthy.

The power of the spiritual matrix would somehow have to be destroyed but in a way that left people's freedom of choice intact. Of course God could have forcibly blasted it away, but He was not interested in any plan that would diminish people's dominion of the earth in any way. He would have to gain entrance to the spiritual matrix somehow, even though Jesus had no sin within Him. He needed a sting operation. He would have to destroy the matrix from within and as a human being exercising human dominion, not as a sovereign God taking control. Jesus's first task, however, was convincing people that God could be trusted.

The Heart of God Revealed

The biggest challenge Jesus faced while on Earth was communicating the heart of the Father God to human beings. While we were originally created in His image, we fell out of the intimate knowledge of Him, and our memory of Him became distorted and dim. Jesus wanted us to know how God feels about us and what His intentions are toward us. He knew that generations of living under the results of the Fall had left us hurting, confused, distrustful, and doubting. He wanted us to be completely confident and able to trust God always. He knew that words and explanations, no matter how artfully given, would not be able to unlock our understanding in any lasting way. Being trapped in the physical dimension, we would need to experience God's intentions for us in some type of tangible way.

One of Jesus's first actions when He "went public" was to

announce God's intentions to us. He openly declared what God sent Him to Earth to do. He was at the synagogue in His hometown of Nazareth on the Sabbath day (day of rest and worship). He was handed the scroll of the Book of Isaiah, a prophet of the Old Testament. He deliberately turned to Isaiah chapter 61 and read the first few verses:

> The Spirit of the Lord [is] upon Me, because He has anointed Me [the Anointed One, the Messiah] to preach the good news (the Gospel) to the poor; He has sent Me to announce release to the captives and recovery of sight to the blind, to send forth as delivered those who are oppressed [who are downtrodden, bruised, crushed, and broken down by calamity], to proclaim the accepted and acceptable year of the Lord [the day when salvation and the free favors of God profusely abound].
> —Luke 4:18–19, AMP

He then rolled up the scroll and told those gathered in the synagogue, "Today this Scripture has been fulfilled while you are present and hearing" (Luke 4:21, AMP).

What did Jesus mean by saying these words? What was He announcing? First, He was clearly telling them that He had come to literally fulfill the words of this prophecy by Isaiah, made seven hundred years before He was born. He indicated that the prophecy was now happening while they were hearing. Jesus also stated that He was not fulfilling the prophecy in His own ability but through God's Spirit of life. He was working in partnership with God's Spirit, who was giving Him power to do certain things. What type of things? Let's take a moment and look at each statement and what it means.

Good news: freedom from bondage

First and foremost, He was here to preach the good news to the poor. The good news was the pronouncement that the kingdom of God was near and that the way back into the spirit dimension was being reopened. The poor He was referring to are not primarily the materially impoverished but the spiritually impoverished. That is, those people who are ready for transformation, ready to admit that they cannot fix themselves and the world. They are people who want to change direction and reconnect with God. They know that continuing to do their own thing will only produce more futility, frustration, and dissatisfaction. They know there must be something "more," something "better," and they are willing to repent of their rebellion against God and return to Him.

Jesus wanted us to know that God was offering release from bondage, from the captivity of Satan's spiritual matrix. This meant that people could get unplugged from the deceptions and manipulations in the spiritual matrix. They could get "deprogrammed" from past hurts and wounds caused by the unjust actions of others. They could delete repetitive thoughts and feelings of failure, fear, and low self-esteem. They did not have to drag around these thoughts and feelings like a ball and chain always weighing them down and diminishing their happiness. They could be completely free!

Recovery of spirit sight

This also meant that people no longer had to stumble blindly in darkness, separated from God and His absolute life. They did not have to keep striving to find meaning and purpose in life without God. The endless chase of following one false path after another, always thinking they were getting somewhere and always finding themselves back at square one, was over. They did not have to keep retracing their steps back to disappointment and disillusionment. Jesus was saying that people could get transformed and reprogrammed to "see" the spirit dimension again. Their spiritual sight could be recovered. People could once again be reinstated to know their purpose. They could exercise their original authority and power. They could experience the deep sense of satisfaction and fulfillment they were created to know.

Complete restoration

Jesus announced deliverance to all those who are damaged by evil (calamity) in any way. This could be people who are emotionally hurt or betrayed, people who find themselves stuck in recurring patterns of negative emotions like despair, depression, anger, or anxiety. This could also be people who are suffering from poverty, illness, natural calamities like earthquakes or hurricanes, or man-made disasters like war or terrorism. Jesus is saying that people who are damaged by evil can be delivered from that damage. Their lives can be restored to wholeness and joy. They don't have to try to cope with the scars left by the impact of evil for the rest of their lives.

Jesus proclaimed that God was announcing the acceptable year of the Lord, when His free favors profusely abound. What did

Jesus mean? This statement meant a lot more to His hearers two thousand years ago than it does to us today. Under the Law given by God, all debts were to be canceled and zeroed out every seven years, and every fifty years all property was to be redistributed to the original families who owned it. This was called the year of Jubilee, or the acceptable year of the Lord, when everything was returned to its original state of ownership. In establishing this practice, the Law became a picture of the promise of restoration that God made to Adam and Eve after the Fall. Everything would be returned to its original state. Here Jesus was declaring that it was now time for the fulfillment of God's promise to reverse the curse. The time had come to open the door for us to be restored to our original position of authority and dominion. This was an incredible pronouncement!

Demonstrating the Promise

As promising as His words were, they were, after all, only words. But was there any concrete evidence of reality behind the words? Jesus knew that people needed more than a description of restoration and kingdom living. They needed to see that the kingdom of God was present and among them as He claimed. So Jesus demonstrated the power and authority of the kingdom every day. He healed all who came to Him seeking healing and believing they would receive it. The Bible indicates that multitudes came to Him to be healed and that He never turned anyone away. They were all healed, most of them instantly. These healings included all types of illnesses and disorders; many people who were healed had been chronically ill for a long time. In some cases the healings involved restoration of withered or missing limbs, sight, or hearing. Other cases involved emotional healing and even restoration to sanity.

Healing was one major way Jesus demonstrated the power and authority of the kingdom of God to restore people. But He also demonstrated kingdom authority over the natural elements. He quieted a storm on a large lake, walked on water, made food multiply to feed a large crowd in a deserted place, and turned water to wine at a marriage feast to save the host from public embarrassment. We call these events miracles because they are far from the way things ordinarily happen in the physical dimension. We see them rarely, if at all, and even when we do see or hear of them, we are not sure we can believe it. We are so dominated by the limited knowledge our five senses can capture that anything out of line with the physical dimension seems preposterous to us. Jesus wanted to broaden our perspective, to pull back the curtain on the spirit dimension and let us see what life in that dimension looks like. He wanted to demonstrate that God was inviting us back into that dimension, even though we no longer remembered that it truly exists. He had to let us know it was real, and it was God's intention to restore it to us. God's heart was to return everything to us we lost in the Fall. He was reversing the curse and extending once again the opportunity to partner with Him and be part of His family.

Through His words and daily actions Jesus was effectively demonstrating God's feelings and intentions to us. But how would He prove to us that we could have complete confidence and trust in God?

love Is Not a four-letter Word

I hope you saw the vintage movie *Star Wars*.[1] It was a wonderfully made movie that set the standard for sci-fi stories of outer space. If you saw it, you will remember the bar scene where Luke Skywalker, Obi-Wan Kenobe, Han Solo, and Chewbacca met to cut an interstellar transportation deal. The bar is filled with wonderfully strange creatures from all sorts of galaxies, which definitely gave the scene an "otherworldly" feel. However, once I got past their strange appearances, I was struck with how remarkably humanlike the creatures were behaving in their greetings, conversations, disagreements, and conflicts. Except for their unusual looks, it could have been a bar scene from an old western. I realized then that although we can conceive of creatures looking very different from us, we are limited in our ability to understand the inner workings of any creature other than ourselves. So how can we possibly understand the motives of the divine ET, a being of absolute life who is spirit?

The Bible says that God does not have love but that He is love. We all have some working definition of what we mean by *love*. But do any of us know what love truly is, and have any of us ever really experienced love? Although this is a familiar word to us—we love a friend, as a parent we love our child, we have sexual love for our spouse—we still have a limited understanding of love. For God uses the word *love* in a unique sense, one that is difficult to capture in human words. The God kind of love is unlike anything we have ever experienced. It is totally "other focused." It does not worry about "What's in it for me?" or "Am I being taken for granted?" This love gives and gives, never keeping score or counting the cost.

It seeks the good of the other and is willing to forgo its own gratification to see that others get what they desire.

An early follower of Jesus, the apostle Paul, gave us this description in 1 Corinthians chapter 13:

> Love is patient, love is kind. It does not envy, it does not boast, it is not proud. It is not rude, it is not self-seeking, it is not easily angered, it keeps no record of wrongs. Love does not delight in evil but rejoices with the truth. It always protects, always trusts, always hopes, always perseveres. Love never fails.
>
> —1 Corinthians 13:4–8

Can you imagine someone loving you this way, always being patient and kind with you, never throwing your past mistakes up to you, always protecting you and never failing you? The Bible describes God as love and repeatedly declares that God loves us. So someone does love you this way, and that someone is God. About now you might be thinking, "Yeah, that sounds good on paper, but where's the proof? How can I ever believe a statement like that?"

love Demonstrated

The proof is in the life and especially the death of Jesus. Remember Jesus was God taking on humanity and limiting Himself to living a human life. Though a physical person like us, He walked in the spirit dimension and displayed the power and authority over the physical dimension that we were originally given. He welcomed all types of people equally. He respected them and shared with them the good news about God reversing the curse and inviting human beings back into partnership. He untangled good and evil and displayed pure goodness to people. In everything He did and said He modeled God's intentions. His words and deeds made Him enormously popular among the common people. And in return for all this, He was violently murdered.

You see, Jesus's popularity made some leaders, especially the religious ones, uneasy and possibly a little jealous. They feared that there might be a political uprising, and they had a lot to lose if the status quo was interrupted. Besides, they didn't agree with Jesus's theology and were more than a little offended by His evaluation of them. So they plotted about how to get rid of Him and found that one of His disciples could be bribed to betray Him. They arranged to take Him into custody in secret, at night, away from the crowds. They tried Him in a hastily convened tribunal, again at night, with false witnesses paid to lie. They trumped up a case against Him and then turned Him over to Roman authorities, because only the Romans had the right of capital punishment.

If you saw *The Passion of the Christ*, you witnessed Jesus's last twenty-four hours before dying depicted in graphic and gory detail. Why did Jesus do it? Why did He allow Himself to be brutalized in that way? Crucifixion was probably one of the cruelest and most torturous deaths ever devised. It was designed to be slow and agonizingly painful. A person hanging on a cross had to fight for every breath, pushing up with their feet, and then letting their weight fall against the spikes through their wrists, sending spasms of pain through their body. Death could take days as the lungs slowly filled with fluid and their hearts began to fail due to the prolonged physical stress. And though Jesus is always shown modestly in a loincloth, the truth is that people were crucified totally nude. They had to endure that humiliation in addition to the physical torture.

The Bible makes it clear that Jesus could have called thousands of angels to His defense and saved Himself. (See Matthew 26:53.) He didn't have to subject Himself to the humiliation and torture. So why did He? Although the religious leaders were motivated by jealousy and political concerns to eliminate Jesus, His death was not merely the result of a conspiracy to kill Him. This may have been what was going on in the physical dimension, but much, much more was going on in the spirit dimension. The Bible gives us a hint in Hebrews 12:2: "He, for the joy [of obtaining the prize] that was set before Him, endured the cross, despising and ignoring the shame, and is now seated at the right hand of the throne of God" (AMP).

What possible "joy" can there be in torture and death? And what was the prize set before Jesus? What was going on in the spirit dimension in Jesus's death on the cross? To understand the spiritual significance of Jesus's death, we need to look at how God describes His relationship with us long before Jesus came to Earth by using His prophets to speak His promises to the Jews. Two important prophets in the Old Testament, Isaiah and Jeremiah, prophesied about God's intentions in relating to us. The prophet Isaiah says this about God's regard for us:

> My love and kindness shall not depart from you, nor shall
> My covenant of peace and completeness be removed, says
> the Lord, Who has compassion on you.
> —Isaiah 54:10, AMP

In Jeremiah 31:3 God states:

I have loved you with an everlasting love; I have drawn you with loving-kindness.

And again in Jeremiah 33:11 (AMP), the prophet reminds us of God's promise:

Give praise and thanks to the Lord of hosts, for the Lord is good; for His mercy and kindness and steadfast love endure forever! For I will cause the captivity of the land to be reversed and return to be as it was at first, says the Lord.

Remember that people were separated from God's presence, trapped in the limitations of the physical dimension and under the deception of the spiritual matrix. They were often unwitting pawns to Satan's manipulations. Additionally, they were invaded by that hideous spiritual virus, the sin principle, as a result of rebelling against God. This virus invaded all people everywhere and resulted in physical death and all types of evil, destruction, and disaster. The Bible states simply, "For the wages of sin is death" (Romans 6:23), and "For all have sinned and fall short of the glory of God" (Romans 3:23).

What did Jesus's death accomplish in the spirit dimension? What was the joy, the prize Jesus gained through dying on the cross? We will look at this "mystery of the ages" in the next chapter.

⁊(7)ᴸ

THE DIVINE STING:
THE MYSTERY OF
THE AGES REVEALED

God originally taught Adam and Eve that they could impart life to cover their sin by shedding the life force, the blood, of another living being, an animal. Later, as part of the Law given to the Israelites through Moses (remember the leader whom God used to free the Israelites from slavery in Egypt?), God explained more fully:

> For the life of a creature is in the blood, and I have given it to you to make atonement [covering] for yourselves on the altar; it is the blood that makes atonement [covering] for one's life.
>
> —Leviticus 17:11

Based on this, people continued to sacrifice to cleanse themselves from sin, but no animal blood could overturn and destroy the power of sin. No animal sacrifice could reverse the curse. Only God's absolute life could disarm sin and make it powerless.

That absolute life of God was in Jesus. God was His Father. He was a human being, but a human being uncontaminated by the sin virus. And He willingly chose to follow God's Spirit of life and not do His own thing. As He approached His death sentence on the cross, He approached His ultimate purpose in coming to Earth: to reverse the curse of sin and death. God's unchanging love for us compelled Him to make the ultimate sacrifice: His own life! The Bible explains it this way:

> In this [the cross] the love of God was made manifest (displayed) where we are concerned: in that God sent His Son [Jesus], the only begotten or unique [Son], into the world so that we might live through Him. In this is love: not that we loved God, but that He loved us and sent His Son [Jesus] to be the propitiation (the atoning sacrifice) for our sins.
>
> —1 John 4:9–10, AMP

The Second Passover

Jesus was crucified during the feast of Passover. I hope you remember from chapter 4 the description of the Passover event in which God delivered the Jews from slavery in Egypt. Each family had to take a healthy, perfect lamb, sacrifice it, and put its blood on the top and sides of their doors. The blood was a sign they were under God's protection, and the death angel did not enter their house but passed over it. Jesus had lived a perfect life. There was no sin in Him. His blood contained His life force, the absolute life of God, because He lived in complete partnership with His Father God. His blood contained the ability to absolutely destroy the power of sin and death. His blood could and did reverse the curse!

Without realizing what they were doing in plotting to kill Jesus, the religious leaders were offering up the perfect Lamb, the Son of God Himself. He was the final sacrifice that dismantled the curse of sin and death. The door to the spirit dimension, the opportunity to reconnect with God, and the way to regain our dominion on Earth were all being reopened to us. The Bible states:

> But because of his great love for us, God, who is rich in mercy, made us alive with Christ [Jesus] even when we were dead in transgressions [sin]—it is by grace you have been saved [from the curse of sin and death]. And God raised us up with Christ [Jesus] and seated us with him in the heavenly realms [the spirit dimension]…in order that in the coming ages he might show the incomparable riches of his grace, expressed in his kindness to us in Christ Jesus.
> —Ephesians 2:4–7

The Great Exchange

What made Jesus's death so powerful was not just that His blood was shed but that an eternal exchange took place in the spirit dimension. Jesus not only died, but He also took upon Himself all sin and death. All the calamity, all the destruction of evil that would ever happen in the world, He took into Himself. This means all the suffering, pain, and heartache caused by conflict, wars, sickness, failed relationships, poverty, starvation, and every sad or bad thing you can imagine. It was as if He sucked all the darkness of evil into Himself. He bore the weight of this collected evil physically, mentally, emotionally, and spiritually. He even experienced spiritual death (separation from His Father God) for the first time in His existence. This was so excruciatingly painful for Him that He cried out, "My God, my God, why have you forsaken me?" as He died on the cross (Matthew 27:46). Second Corinthians 5:21 tells us, "God made him [Jesus] who had no sin to be sin for us."

Jesus's suffering was much greater than the physical agony and torture Mel Gibson portrayed so well in *The Passion of the Christ*. It went light-years beyond physical suffering. Hundreds of years earlier, the Old Testament prophet Isaiah prophesied the suffering of Jesus by describing it this way:

> Surely He has borne our griefs (sicknesses, weaknesses, and distresses) and carried our sorrows and pains [of punishment], yet we [ignorantly] considered Him stricken, smitten, and afflicted by God [as if with leprosy]. But He was wounded for our transgressions, He was bruised for our guilt and iniquities; the chastisement [needful to

obtain] peace and well-being for us was upon Him, and with the stripes [that wounded] Him we are healed and made whole. All we like sheep have gone astray, we have turned every one to his own way; and the Lord has made to light upon Him *[Jesus]* the guilt and iniquity of us all.

—Isaiah 53:4–6, AMP

There are no human words that can begin to capture the massive suffering of Jesus. Why did He do it? The answer is simple. The answer is love.

But God demonstrates his own love for us in this: While we were still sinners, Christ died for us.

—Romans 5:8

I heard a story recently about a young soldier returning from the war in Iraq. He was involved in the prolonged siege at Fallujah. An incident happened that radically changed his life. In going house to house, he and a friend entered a house where a terrorist armed with a suicide bomb awaited them. Without hesitation his friend threw himself on the terrorist, saving the young soldier's life by blocking the impact of the bomb with his body. After that young soldier returned home, a friend invited him to a church service where the minister described Jesus's sacrificial death on the cross in much the same way as I have explained it to you in this chapter. After the service, the young soldier commented to the minister, "I don't see what makes Jesus so unique. My friend died for me in Iraq. He did the same thing as Jesus." The minister replied, "Your friend did a very brave and noble thing giving his life to save you. But that is not the same as what Jesus did. Had your friend stripped the bomb off the terrorist and fallen on it to save the life of that terrorist, then that would be the same thing that Jesus did for us. He gave His life for us when we were still enemies and in complete rebellion."

You see, Jesus went to the cross and took on the evil we let into the world when we were still going our own way in rebellion. We were not seeking Him. We were still wandering around in spiritual darkness trying to make our life work without Him. He made His incredible sacrifice, knowing that some of us would still reject His love. But His love for us was so great that He didn't consider it a waste. He considered it a joy to offer us our freedom whether or not we would choose to accept His gift. He wanted us to get the message that He loves us and wants to reconnect with us.

The next time you see a cross, let the divine ET, God, talk to you. Hear what He is saying: "I love you. You are so important to Me that I wanted to make a way for us to be connected again. I don't want you to be blinded by sin, struggling against evil and feeling angry or hopeless. I don't want your life to be spent wandering in darkness, chasing one unrealized dream after another. I don't want you to experience the empty void inside when you do get the success you crave and it leaves you still feeling frustrated and unsatisfied. I want to set you free from the bondage and deception of Satan's spiritual matrix. I want your life to be fulfilling and full of hope and joy. I want you to trust Me and have total confidence in My love and goodwill to you. I want you to reenter the spirit dimension and regain the power and authority I gave you in Eden. I want you to partner and reign in the heavens with Me. I wanted all this so much that I became one of you and lived among you for thirty-three years. I demonstrated in My life what you were originally created to be. I took all the darkness and evil that could ever plague you into Myself. I neutralized its power through My blood that I willingly shed for you. Never, never forget how valuable you are to Me and how much I love you."

The Sting

Jesus's death canceled the penalty of sin and the evil we let into the world in the Fall. But it took another action to completely reverse the curse. It was an action that looked like a total defeat, but it snatched out of seeming annihilation a total and eternal victory. You are aware of sting operations and how they are set up. In the end, a sting operation "works" because it looks like something it is not. It catches its intended target on his home turf doing what he ordinarily does because it looks like business as usual. The target does not suspect the undercover plot that is going on. A contemporary example of this would be the undercover narcotics sting in which a dealer is selling drugs to a narcotics agent posing as a drug buyer.

The Matrix Revolutions, the final movie in the Matrix trilogy, ends with a sting operation. There is a scene where Neo and Agent Smith (the untiring machine clone) face off in a mortal combat in front of hundreds of Agent Smith dittos. They have a prolonged and very impressive martial arts duel, but in the end Neo is being pulverized by nonstop blows from Smith. Agent Smith begins taunting Neo, "Why, Mr. Anderson? Why do you do it? Why get up? Why keep fighting?...Can you tell me what it is?...Why, Mr. Anderson? Why? Why do you persist?" Beaten into a near stupor, Neo gets up, staggers forward, and, looking at Smith, replies, "Because I choose to."[1]

This response is ludicrous to Smith's machinelike logic that sees the impossibility of success for Neo in the situation. He shouts back through clenched teeth, his face contorted with rage, "This is my world, my world!" Smith digs his hand into Neo's neck, and a machine veneer begins to envelope Neo. Smith asks Neo, "Is it over?" And Neo nods his head yes as his metamorphosis into a Smith clone is complete.[2] For a moment it looks like it is indeed over and that the machines have prevailed. But suddenly the Neo-turned-Smith explodes violently as if blown apart by a force from within. The original Smith also explodes, and all the Smith dittos begin exploding as well. The determination of will, the choice to resist the Matrix, became so strong in Neo that it imploded the machine-made Matrix from the inside out. In the end, Neo became one with the Matrix, and from his union with the Matrix he overcame and destroyed it. Smith could never have anticipated this outcome. He was caught in the sting and wiped out.[3]

In a somewhat similar manner, Jesus had to become a part of Satan's spiritual matrix in order to neutralize its power over us. And He had to do this in such a way that He preserved our integrity as beings with free wills and our legal right of dominion on the earth. God had promised in Eden that a human, the seed of the woman, would come and crush Satan's head. I'm sure down through the centuries Satan had been carefully surveying the human race. He was trying to spot this promised person and destroy him or her before they could do any damage. Probably the last thing Satan imagined was that God would take on humanity and come and live among us. In doing this, God began an under-cover sting that would eventually collapse Satan's dominion.

We do know that Satan was alerted to Jesus's presence and that he did try to destroy Jesus several times, beginning when Jesus was a baby. Satan moved a jealous king to murder all the male babies under two years of age in Bethlehem in an attempt to eliminate Jesus. But God warned His parents in a dream, and they left for Egypt and stayed there until that king died. So they weren't even in Bethlehem when the slaughter occurred. Several times after Jesus began traveling, teaching, and doing signs and wonders, Satan provoked people to try to take His life. On one occasion a crowd tried to push Him off a cliff, but He simply walked away. (See Luke 4:28–30.) Satan also personally tempted Jesus and offered Him all the kingdoms in the world if He would only bow down and worship him. In essence Satan was saying, "I'll give You anything and everything You could want here on Earth if You will only worship me." Unlike Adam and Eve, Jesus did not fall for Satan's deception. He continued to follow His Father God.

We know that Satan was involved in the plot to capture and kill Jesus, because he manipulated Jesus's disciple Judas into betraying Him. The Bible tells us that Jesus gathered with His disciples to celebrate Passover. While they were still eating, Satan entered into and took possession of Judas, and Jesus said to Judas, "What you are going to do, do quickly." And Judas left immediately to betray Him. (See John 13:27–30.) Satan may have expected that Jesus would defend Himself. He must have been surprised but delighted that Jesus was sentenced to death and offered no resistance. After all, he was looking for the human who would defeat him. If he could get rid of Jesus, he could eliminate this threat.

Damnation Damned

When Jesus died under the weight of sin and evil, He entered hell. This is the region of the damned—those who have chosen to be forever separated from God. Hell contains the gates of the spiritual matrix, the seat of Satan's domain. For a brief moment Satan probably thought he had won and eliminated the prophesied threat to his dominion forever. But Satan miscalculated. By engineering the death of Jesus and admitting Him to hell, he had not captured and contained Him as he anticipated. Instead, he had unwittingly allowed the one man into his headquarters who was filled with the absolute life of God. He had opened his domain to the life that could eradicate in an instant all the power structures Satan had been erecting for thousands of years to enslave humans. If Satan hadn't been so eager to snatch victory, he might have seen the divine sting unfolding. But his own pride became his greatest enemy and, in the end, his downfall. The Bible makes it very clear that God's undercover operation was a sting, calling it "divine wisdom" and a "mystery hidden for the ages." It declares in 1 Corinthians 2:7–8:

> No, we speak of God's secret wisdom, a wisdom that has been hidden and that God destined for our glory before time began. None of the rulers of this age [Satan and his demons] understood it, for if they had, they would not have crucified the Lord of glory [Jesus].

Jesus foreshadowed the mystery, the divine sting, several times shortly before His death.

> Now is the time for judgment on this world; now the prince of this world [Satan] will be driven out.
> —John 12:31

> I have told you now before it happens, so that when it does happen you will believe. I will not speak with you much longer, for the prince of this world [Satan] is coming. He has no hold on me.
> —John 14:29–30

> The prince of this world now stands condemned.
> —John 16:11

Jesus knew the planned outcome of the undercover operation. Therefore, He could look at His death on the cross and look past His suffering to the joy of executing the perfect sting on Satan—a sting that would annihilate his seat of power and set humans free.

Death, Where Is Your Sting?

Years after Jesus's death, one of His followers, the apostle Paul, wrote about the defeat of Satan and the destruction of his dominion this way:

> Since the children [humans] have flesh and blood, he [Jesus] too shared in their humanity so that by his death he might destroy him who holds the power of death—that

is, the devil—and free those who all their lives were held
in slavery by their fear of death.

—Hebrews 2:14–15

[God] disarmed the principalities and powers *[Satan and
his demons]* that were ranged against us and made a bold
display and public example of them, in triumphing over
them in Him *[Jesus]* and in it [the cross].

—Colossians 2:15, AMP

But how do we know that the sting operation was successful?
We have one absolutely ironclad piece of evidence: the resurrection of Jesus on the third day after He was crucified. He totally
reversed the curse of sin and death. The absolute life within Him
absolutely blew death and hell wide open! Not only was He seen
by His inner circle of disciples, but He also appeared on various
occasions to at least five hundred people before leaving Earth.
By conquering death and returning to Earth in the resurrection,
Jesus wanted to make it clear that death is not the end. Death
has no ultimate power over us. Jesus said, "…[I am living in
the eternity of the eternities]. I died, but see, I am alive forev-
ermore; and I possess the keys of death and Hades (the realm of
the dead)" (Revelation 1:18, AMP). He wanted us to know that He,
not Satan, now holds death. There is no more reason to fear. The
Bible declares:

For this perishable [part of us] must put on the imperishable [nature], and this mortal [part of us, this nature that is
capable of dying] must put on immortality (freedom from
death). And when this perishable puts on the imperishable
and this that was capable of dying puts on freedom from

death, then shall be fulfilled the Scripture that says, Death is swallowed up (utterly vanquished forever) in and unto victory. O death, where is your victory? O death, where is your sting?

—1 Corinthians 15:53–55, AMP

His disciples had all been frightened and had run away after His capture. But they discovered this freedom from fear and became bold and determined after His resurrection. They spent the rest of their lives sharing the good news of the kingdom of God, "unplugging" all the people they met who chose to repent and leave the deceptions of Satan's spiritual matrix. Like the resistance fighters in *The Matrix*, Jesus's followers faced danger and opposition from people still plugged into the spiritual matrix. These people were under the deception of Satan and fought against their message of the kingdom of God. But they persisted in telling anyone who would listen about God's invitation back into the spirit dimension, back into partnership with Him. Sometimes it cost them their lives, but they persisted anyway. They knew that if people would listen and believe the good news, then they would choose to unplug from the spiritual matrix of Satan. They would begin to experience the freedom, hope, joy, and fulfillment that God originally intended for them to have.

Your Choice: Reality or Deception

If this good news is really the truth, you may be wondering, "Why isn't there more evidence of the kingdom of God here on

Earth?" This is an excellent question. Although defeated and stripped of his power over humans, Satan did not die and go away. He is still here, and he is still deceiving multitudes. Those who continue to stay plugged into his spiritual matrix live in his virtual reality world of stealth and deception. Although he has no true power over them, if they listen to and believe his lies, then he can use this false belief system to manipulate them to accomplish his purposes. Their situation reminds me of a newscast I heard as a child. It was twenty-five years or so after World War II had ended. The story was about a Japanese soldier who had just been captured; he had been hiding out all that time on one of the Pacific islands. He was completely cut off from the rest of the world and thought the war was still going on, so he was hiding in resistance. He had no idea that the war was over, that we were at peace with Japan, and that he could have returned to his homeland and family years earlier. A false belief system had robbed him of years of his life and enjoyment while he stayed hiding in fear.

Never forget that Satan is our primary adversary and that his agenda is to steal, kill, and destroy us. Wherever you see death and destruction on Earth, you can be sure that Satan is present and working. People who are still plugged into his spiritual matrix are opening themselves and the world around them to Satan's strategies and plans.

God's ultimate purpose was to open the spirit dimension back up to us and to invite us to regain our original dominion and authority. But God respects our free will and our legal right to decide what happens to us here on Earth. Our lives are truly our domain. He will not force anything on us. He loves us and will not coerce us in any way. He has done everything He can to make a way and offer His invitation to us. But each of us must make the choice to accept or reject His offer. Our decision will affect our entire life and touch everyone and everything around us. We truly hold the wild card in our hands. The most important question is, what will we do with it?

⤜(8)⤛

ENCOUNTER WITH THE DIVINE ET: THE RED PILL OR THE BLUE PILL

You take the blue pill, the story ends, you...believe whatever you want to believe. You take the red pill, you stay in [reality], and I show you how deep the rabbit hole goes. Remember, all I'm offering is the truth, nothing more..."[1]

In the movie *The Matrix*, these words are spoken by

Morpheus, a leader of the resistance fighters, to Neo at the end of their first encounter. Neo has been told about the Matrix, but in order to truly understand, he must experience it firsthand. He must go through the transformation process of unplugging from the Matrix and being deprogrammed. He must learn about life in the real world outside the Matrix. Morpheus holds out his hand that contains two pills: one red and the other blue. The red pill will take Neo in a bold new direction, into a dimension he has never experienced before. It will reveal the illusory world of the Matrix for what it really is. It will transform Neo and significantly change his life forever. The blue pill will allow him to return back to his current life in the Matrix, with no memory of what has transpired. He will be swallowed back into the virtual reality of the Matrix and live his life as an energy cell of the AI machines that determine his destiny. There are only two choices. There is no neutral third position available. Neo chooses the red pill and begins the greatest adventure of his life as he discovers power and authority he never had in the Matrix.

In the first chapter of this book, I invited you to actively engage in what you read here and to anticipate a true encounter with the divine ET. I don't have two pills to offer you, but I do have a critical choice point. It is the choice between two ways of living and being in the world. One is life: God's Spirit of life and reentry into the spirit dimension. The other is death: continued separation from God and life, in ongoing bondage to Satan's delusions in the spiritual matrix. Just as Neo had only two choices, so do you. There is no neutral third position. You cannot do your own thing and run your own world. The rebellion already has a leader. His name is Satan, and he will never allow you any freedom. He only knows how to dominate.

Just like Neo, if you choose life, you will radically change the way you understand and live your life. You will never be the same. You will begin the greatest adventure of your life as you learn to experience a whole new dimension of reality—a spiritual dimension. You can have an ongoing encounter with the being who set the universe in motion. You can rediscover your authority and rightful dominion here on Earth. Or you can back away and choose to continue the status quo. You can live your life the best you can within the confines of the spiritual matrix and the limitations of the physical dimension. You know this option. You have already been living your life this way. Go this way, and you can expect more of what you are already experiencing as long as you are here on Earth.

The Invitation From Another World

God does not coerce or bribe you. He will not manipulate you. He has offered you the truth, nothing more. The truth is that He loves you. He wants ongoing dialogue with you. He wants to reinstate you to your full position of authority and power. He wants to return you to the type of authority and power that originates in the spirit dimension so you can exercise your rightful dominion in the physical dimension here on Earth. He wants to give you peace, love, and joy. He wants your life to be meaningful, fulfilling, and satisfying. He wants to fill your life with positive relationships with others who will believe in you, encourage you, love you, and challenge you.

God has proven His intentions to you. He loved you so much that He became humanity and came to Earth to demonstrate to you what you were originally created to be. Love for you led Him to take on your sin and failings and die on a cross in terrible agony. He went into hell and blew it wide apart for your sake so He could seize the keys of hell and death from Satan. He did this to set you free from the bondage of the spiritual matrix and fear. He reversed the curse of sin and death for you. He bids you come and let Him show you who you truly are. Let Him teach you how to coreign with Him in heavenly places.

What He asks from you in return is simple. Of your own free will He wants you to choose the Spirit of life. He wants you to choose to depart from going your own way and desire to return to relationship with Him. This is a radical act in which you decide to turn from your present way of being, thinking, and doing in the world. You become open to being transformed into a new reality. You do not have to do the transforming; in fact, you can't. He will transform you, but only if you are willing and if you ask Him to have an encounter with you. This action is called repentance, and it simply means that you admit that your current way of being, thinking, and doing is not working that well. You are ready for change. You have given up thinking you can change yourself by sheer willpower. You believe He loves you, and you want Him to encounter you and transform you.

Don't worry about who you are and what you've done or not done in life. In His eyes we have all missed the original mark we were created for, because we have all rebelled and tried to make life work on our own terms. It doesn't matter if you are a business executive, a student, a homemaker, a call girl, a drug addict, a gang member, or a prisoner on death row. God loves you. He does not condemn you. He will not shame you or load you with guilt if you come to Him. God is not interested in demeaning you and making you feel bad for how you may be living. He wants to embrace you and welcome you back home. He wants to share His absolute life with you. He wants to give you hope about your future. He wants to fill your life with good things. He wants you to be confident about your identity and to know your purpose on Earth.

The Bible says:

> For God so loved the world [that's you!] that he gave his one and only Son [Jesus], that whoever believes in him [Jesus] should not perish [be under the curse of sin and death] but have eternal life [God's absolute life!]. For God did not send his Son [Jesus] into the world to condemn the world, but to save the world through him [Jesus].
>
> —John 3:16–17

God's Favorite Love Story

Jesus frequently told stories to people to help them understand what He was trying to teach them. The following story is one I think He told frequently to people because it so beautifully illustrates the heart of the Father God. It is about family restoration and the unchanging love of a father for his child. (I've updated it a little.)

There was a very wealthy man who had two sons. When his younger son reached adulthood, he was eager to leave home and go do his own thing. He began to ask his father for his inheritance.

Although he was not legally entitled to his inheritance until his father died, the father gave it to him early because he kept asking and asking. The father hoped his younger son would stay and help him manage the family estate. But he could see that his younger son was determined to leave. So with great sadness the father said good-bye, and the younger son left home.

At first the younger son had a great time. He had lots of money, and he traveled and partied all the time. He eventually settled in a distant large city that was known for its trendy social circles and nightlife. He leased a luxurious penthouse suite and soon was the hub of social activity. Everybody who was anybody came to his lavish parties. But on his own he made some critical mistakes. Without his father's wise counsel to guide him, he foolishly squandered his wealth on his lifestyle. He also made ill-advised business decisions. He got involved with some high-risk investment schemes that went bust and eventually was completely broke and had to declare bankruptcy.

He lost his penthouse suite, his car, and virtually everything except the clothes on his back. His trendy friends, who couldn't get enough of him when he was throwing parties, were now nowhere to be seen. To make matters even worse, the economy had gone into a recession, and the job market was really tight. He couldn't even get a foot in the door for an interview because of his poor credit history. In desperation he finally took a manual labor job on a farm located in the country some distance from the large city.

There he was totally alone. One of his jobs was feeding the animals. He made only minimum wage, and sometimes toward the end of the month he would run out of money. He discovered that the cornmeal mash he fed the hogs, although not tasty, was palatable, and when he had no money left, he would eat the hogs' mash. One day when he was eating hog food, he started thinking about his father and how good he had it at home. But he knew he was a failure and felt really ashamed of himself. Besides, he had blown his inheritance and had no right to expect his father to welcome him back. Over the next few months he kept thinking about his father and home. He realized that his father's farm workers were paid more than he was currently earning and had better benefits. He thought to himself, "At least if I go home, I could get a job from my father on his farm and live better than I'm living here."

So he quit his job and hitchhiked back to his father's home. While traveling he kept rehearsing what he would say to his father. He decided to be honest and just admit he had been foolish and squandered his money. He was coming back home because he needed a job, and he hoped his father would give him one. He would not ask for any special favors. He knew he had blown it big time.

It was raining the day the younger son arrived back at his father's home. As he was walking down the long driveway to the estate, he was caught completely by surprise when his father came running up to him and embraced him with tears in his eyes. His father then began repeatedly kissing him all over his face and neck. Before he could say anything, his father took off his own raincoat and threw it around the son's shoulders. He looked directly in his son's eyes and with the warmest smile said, "Thank God you are back home! I've been waiting and hoping every day that you would return. My heart broke with sadness the day you left. I thought I would never see you again. This is the happiest day of my life." He drew the son close and embraced him again.

The son began crying and trying to give his rehearsed speech about blowing it and needing a job. But his father began calling his farmhands and telling them, "Round up and slaughter some of our prizewinning steers and hogs. As soon as the rain stops, get the barbecue pits going. Call all my friends and neighbors and invite them over for a celebration, for my son who was lost has now returned to me." As they walked in the front door together, the son felt something slip on his finger. He looked down to see that his father had taken off his signet ring and slipped it on his hand. The son blinked back more tears in disbelief. His father was giving him back his position as son and heir. As he looked into his father's eyes, he heard his father say, "Welcome home, son."

You can read the Bible version of this story in Luke 15:11–32. I believe that Jesus told this story because He wanted us all to know that God desires reunion with each one of us. It doesn't matter if we are at the pinnacle of success or in the depths of despair. He eagerly awaits our return to relationship with Him. He wants to give us back everything we lost in the Fall. He wants to restore us to our original created place as beings created in His image.

So far in this book I have shared many things with you about God. If you remember only one thing, I hope it will be this story. No matter where you go or what you do, I hope you remember this story of the Father God's love for you. I hope you remember that He desires a restored relationship with you. For this is the simple truth, nothing more.

Close Encounters of the Divine Kind

You may be wondering, "What would an encounter with God, the divine ET, be like? What can I expect? What will happen?" I can tell you, first of all, that no two encounters are alike. You are totally unique, and God will encounter you in a way that will mean the most to you. Sometimes an encounter is very dramatic, with a person hearing or seeing things out of the ordinary. Sometimes nothing external happens, but the person experiences a profound shift internally. He or she suddenly "sees" what was invisible before. Regardless of what happens, everyone who has an encounter knows with certainty they have met the divine ET and that their life will never be the same. While I can't tell you what your encounter will be like, I can share a couple of stories of other people's encounters with the divine ET.

My Personal Divine Encounter

I grew up as a minister's son. I now realize what a blessing that was, although during my childhood I certainly had my doubts. And despite years of sitting in church and hearing about Jesus, very little sunk into me. In fact, when I hit puberty, I developed a very different identity. I was always ready for a good time and early on demonstrated the ability to influence my peers. I became determined to do whatever it took to capture the ultimate "high." For several years I lived for sex, drugs, and rock 'n' roll. I had lots of friends, no shortage of dates, and lots of adventures. But somehow inside, I grew more and more bland and empty. Everything was going my way, and everything was fun. Why did I feel so restless and hollow? I had no idea that God was getting ready to encounter me.

One weekend when I was seventeen, I was at a party at my friend's house. It was the typical scene—you know, parents away for the weekend, lots of beer, plenty of pot, and my friends all milling around eager to party. I was so tired of doing the same party scene that I was on the verge of burnout. I looked around and actually realized I was bored. In the middle of all the activity and noise, I was bored. I left the room where everyone was and went to a vacant bedroom in the back of the house. It was relatively quiet away from all the music and conversation. I was loaded, and my mind started tumbling.

I felt so frustrated. Inside I felt as if I were reaching for something just out of my grasp. What it was I didn't know. I just felt that somehow it must be there. I found myself beginning to talk to God. To this day I remember what I said. In an audible voice I cried out, "God, I don't know if You exist. But if You do exist, and if what my parents told me as a little boy is true, that You died for my sins and that there is a heaven and a hell, I want You to reveal Yourself to me and reveal the truth to me."

It was a cry of sincere seeking coming from my frustration. I don't remember expecting anything, but the moment I uttered those words I felt a surge of warm energy envelop my body. It was a sensation of warmth and love I had never experienced before. At the same moment I felt the incredible warmth, my mind suddenly cleared as if someone had pulled up a window shade.

In a moment I knew that I knew that Jesus was real. His death on the cross was a real event, and His act of love was directed to me.

Stunned, I sat transfixed while one revelation after another flooded me. The first shocking realization to hit me was that the truth of Jesus was always there, in my home, in the church my father pastored. I had been looking everywhere else, including in Eastern religion, for what was right under my nose all along. The second shocking thing was that I was very aware that I was not a good person, and yet God was taking the time to reveal His love to me in such a profound way. I was overwhelmed with how much He loved me, and I wept uncontrollably.

I felt so joyful and excited. All the boredom melted away in the reality of my encounter with Him. I've always been a person of action, and my first impulse was to go back into the front room and tell my friends the incredible revelation I had just received. So I did just that. I marched back to the party and blurted out to everyone, "Guys, I found what we are all looking for. It's Jesus. Jesus revealed Himself to me!" I was ecstatic and beaming. My friends looked at me as if I had smoked one toke of pot too many. My best friend said, "Ché, you have really flipped out this time. But don't worry; you'll be OK tomorrow."

Fortunately for me, what had happened to me was real and not the product of a drug high, as my friend thought. It did not go away the next day or the next or the next. In the midst of that smoky, drug-filled house, nowhere near a cathedral or an altar, as I was sitting alone in a bedroom, God met me. For the next three days, I could not stop weeping. Waves of God's love so gripped me that I could not help but cry. I began telling all my friends what was going on, even though it was difficult to put into words. But it was so good, so positive, so joyful that I wanted to share it with everyone, and I have never stopped. When you encounter God, it is so life changing that you cannot stop talking about it. You have encountered a larger reality, and your life can never be the same.

A Process of Encounter

My encounter with God was internally dramatic and occurred in a moment of time. Sometimes God comes to us in a series of encounters, which we only fully realize when we surrender and respond to Him. God respects our free will and never forces an encounter, but He loves us and offers us repeated opportunities to reconnect. This was the case of a woman I know whom I will call Patti. Patti currently teaches at a university in southern California and is an ardent follower of Jesus. But it wasn't always that way. Here is her story of divine encounter.

Patti grew up in the Northwest. She attended church sporadically and remembers a very vivid dream she had at age six. She saw Jesus on the cross in graphic detail as if she were actually there. Although it was a scene of suffering, she somehow felt at peace and very safe. Years later, when she was about twelve, she looked up at the cross at the front of the church. She suddenly saw Christ crucified on it and heard a voice say to her, "You will discover something someday." While these two events were memorable, Patti didn't give them much thought. Nor did she give God much thought. Church was a place to be socially involved. She didn't pay much attention to stories or sermons.

God was just a word, and she was clueless about what the death of Jesus might mean.

But she was intrigued with the paranormal, and by her early teens she and her friends were dabbling with psychic experiences and white magic. For fun, they got together and chanted and made love potions. Over time they tried séances, and Patti remembers one particularly scary event when a group of them tried to bring back a young boy who had recently died. They were at a slumber party at someone's home. The front door was locked, but an inklike blackness filled the room. The front door swung open, and the dead boy stood there looking confused and then stepped back out. Patti recalls, "It was too much. We all got hysterical and began screaming, and a neighbor called the police." Even though that experience was frightening, Patti and her friends continued periodically to experiment. "Sometimes we'd get really scared and go to the church to pray. The minister there warned us that we should stop because we could get hurt by forces we could not control. We would stop, but then start again. We thought it was fun."

Patti's life drew her away from church after high school. She got married in college, moved to Florida, and became involved in acting in a community theater group. She was enjoying some success getting a few major roles and some write-ups in the local paper. At the same time she found herself once again interested in "spiritual" experiences. She began reading a lot of New Age materials and increasingly getting into nature spirits and crystal power and writing runes to spirits. These experiences with witchcraft led her to decide the spirit world was real, and she was determined to crash into it and get a piece of the action.

One day she was in the middle of setting up a ritual to call spirits forth into her life to help her, when she received a phone call. The caller was a woman who introduced herself and then said she had seen an article about Patti in the local paper and would like to meet her. She said she was in the neighborhood and would like to stop by. Patti relates, "It never occurred to me to ask her how she got my phone number or knew my address. I put my spirit stuff away, and ten minutes later she arrived at my door. I will never forget her. She was very beautiful, over six feet tall, with long dark hair, and dressed completely in white. We had tea and talked about theater, but eventually I talked about my interest in spirits and how you could get them to do favors for you. She said, 'Why would you go to lesser spirits to get things when you could go to the main spirit, God? Can't you believe in something much bigger and vaster than these nature spirits?'"

Patti states, "Her remarks completely upended me. I had never thought about God that way. Although I wasn't sure who God was, from that day on I began praying, I guess, to 'whom it may concern.' But I abandoned witchcraft. I never found out who the woman was. I saw her a couple more isolated times, and then she vanished. No one seemed to know her. Sometimes now I wonder if she was an angel."

While out of her involvement with witchcraft, Patti was still floundering. She kept trying various other New Age practices, especially meditation. One day while in a meditation, she said that suddenly a scene "popped into place." There were rolling green hills and all these white doves on the ground, like a "river of doves." Patti describes following them around a corner and seeing Jesus sitting on a rock. She reports, "I was startled to see Him sitting there in the middle of my meditation. He seemed so real. In fact, this meditation had an immediate reality to it that was different from my other meditations. It felt like I was literally with Him. I asked Him, 'What are You doing here?' He replied, 'I'm waiting for you to get here.' He looked through me and instantly knew everything good and bad about me. But He totally loved me. I looked into His eyes of gentle love and was overwhelmed. I sobbed, throwing myself at His feet. I cried and cried. When I came out of the meditation, I couldn't talk to anyone. I knew what I had experienced was real. I knew Jesus was real. But I still didn't know what to do with this information."

Some years later Patti moved to Southern California. She was going through some difficulties and was stuck at home caring for her mother-in-law, who was ill. There was nothing to do but watch TV. But mysteriously her satellite dish went on the blink, and the only station she could get was a local Christian TV network. While she still remembered her experience with Jesus, Patti had never returned to church and had a rather cynical opinion of religion, especially Christian religion.

She found herself listening to a woman Bible teacher who had a very forthright, no-nonsense approach to the teachings of Jesus. As Patti puts it, "It was the first time I heard anyone teaching about God who made sense. She was having a conference in my area the next month, so I decided to go. I'm so glad I did. For at that meeting I made a decision to surrender, repent, and accept Jesus. As I did, I realized that He had been gently and quietly pursuing me my whole life in one encounter after another. Even though I didn't understand it at the time, He kept patiently inviting me to reconnect with Him. I know on a few occasions He also kept me from making some really bad mistakes and getting involved with evil that was way over my head. I had no idea the fire I was playing with and how close I came to getting burned. I am constantly amazed at how much He loves me."

An Invitation to a Divine Encounter

I could relate many more stories of encounters, all equally interesting. But I can only relate experiences to you—mine and others. I cannot prove the existence or the reality of an encounter with God to you through my words. You must directly experience the divine ET for yourself. It is the only way you will ever know for sure the reality I have described to you. And having your own direct experience beats hearing anyone's story.

Like Morpheus extending his hand containing the red pill and the blue pill to Neo, I can only invite you to open yourself to an encounter with the divine ET. You now stand like Adam and Eve in Eden at the critical choice point. Do you want to have an encounter with God? Do you want to reconnect with your Creator and be restored into a relationship of intimacy with Him? Do you want to rediscover your original destiny in the spirit dimension? Are you willing to surrender doing it your own way and begin learning how to use the power and authority He wants to pour into you through His Spirit of life? Are you tired of always being on your guard and feeling alone? Are you willing to trust His love for you? Are you ready to admit that you can't figure everything out, solve all your problems, and make the world right? Are you willing to let Him lead and guide you? Remember He will never coerce or deceive you. He is inviting you into a love family, a place of belonging and acceptance where you can grow and discover your true identity and fulfillment. Will you say yes to His offer?

There are no set words for encountering God. You can let God know you are open to an encounter in your own words. God waits to be invited into your life. You only need to acknowledge that you want Him to reveal Himself to you, that you believe He exists, and that He will honor your request. You accept His gift of reconciliation, which was Jesus's death on the cross to reverse the curse of sin and death in your life. The words are not that important. The sincerity of your heart is what opens the door to a true encounter. God responds to your sincere desire.

Sometimes people who are not used to talking to God find it helpful to have a guide. I offer this prayer as a guide to an encounter, but remember, there is no formula. Your words, however simple, are just as effective as this prayer.

> *God, I want to know You. I accept Your gift of love to me, the death of Jesus on the cross, and His resurrection that reversed the curse of sin and death in my life. I repent of my rebellion against You and going my own way. I surrender control and give up doing it my way. I want to follow You, God, the rest of my life. I want to reconnect with You and discover my true identity and destiny through Your Spirit of life. I want to have an encounter with You. Please reveal Yourself to me now. Thank You for hearing me and answering my request. Amen.*

It's just this simple, and this is just the beginning. God has a very special gift for you once you seek and experience an encounter with Him. Together we will unwrap that gift in the next chapter.

⑨

THE FORCE IS WITH YOU

I was a young person when the first movie of the Star Wars trilogy came out. Like many other kids my age, I was fascinated by the space-age weaponry, the laser guns and swords, and the incredible power of the Death Star, the intergalactic strategic base of the evil empire. I watched a young man, Luke Skywalker, who represented someone close to my age, take off on the adventure of his life into interstellar space after his home base was raided and his aunt and uncle were killed. Over the course of the three movies, I began to feel I knew Luke and his friends and to some extent the strange, wonderful, and technologically complex world of the future he inhabited.

And in the midst of all this incredible technology and strange creatures from distant galaxies, there was this unseen and indescribable presence called "the Force." The Force could somehow give a person an edge even over space-age technology. It was an ancient element in the universe, imparting skill and wisdom to those who learned how to surrender and "lean into" its guidance. In the first movie, Luke saw this skill modeled in his human mentor, Obi-Wan Kenobe, who also instructed him about the Force. But Obi-Wan Kenobe was killed, and Luke's mediator with the Force was gone.

Luke still sought to understand the Force, and in some ways his quest became more determined in the absence of his mentor. We spent most of the second movie watching Luke learn how to yield to the Force and be guided by it through increasingly complex maneuvers. He had a tutor, Yoda, the little green monk-like creature who frequently reversed his sentence order. But Yoda patiently and wisely counseled Luke as he progressively learned to curb his impulsivity and need to be in control and make his own plans. Yoda let Luke experiment with trying things his own way and experiencing the less-than-desirable results. He knew that Luke's true maturity would come not from being tightly controlled with rules from without but by being yielded to the Force from within.

And we saw that as Luke flowed more freely with the Force, he developed a "sixth sense" that allowed him to detect the presence of danger and to somehow anticipate the moves of others, particularly in combat. He became more aware of another reality and could detect "disturbances in the Force." In the end, it was this alliance with the Force that enabled him to defeat the dark powers of the evil empire.

The Gift of the Divine Force

In some ways Jesus faced a similar situation with His followers. As long as He was physically present with them, He could teach them about the kingdom of God and demonstrate its power and authority. But this left His followers knowing the kingdom from without, and He wanted them to possess it from within. He wanted them to flow with the reality of the kingdom in such a way that they could become a source of life and hope to everyone and everything around them. He knew that developing this ability would require learning and opportunities to experiment and practice. He also knew that as long as He was physically present, His followers would continue to look to Him and not develop their own inner sense of the kingdom.

So He began, even before His death, to speak to them of another One, a divine force, who would come after He left. This One would remain with them forever. This One would teach, guide, counsel, coach, and mentor them. This One would comfort them, give them special discernment, and fill them with joy. This One would reveal mysteries of the spirit dimension to them and give them spiritual authority and power to reclaim their rightful dominion on Earth. This One would be so close to them that He would fill every part of their being with His own essence. This would not be the body-snatching invasion of an alien but the gradual commingling of persons in a partnership over time. This One would not be an impersonal Star Wars Force with a dark as well as a good side. While all pervasive like a force, this One is actually a being of absolute life and light. Jesus called Him the Holy Spirit and stated that He was a divine gift from the Father God.

When He first began to speak to His followers of His departure, I'm sure they were very sad and couldn't imagine how anything could be better than having Jesus with them physically. But at His last supper with them, the night before He was crucified and killed, Jesus spoke extensively to His followers about the gift of the Father to them, the Holy Spirit. He said:

> And I will ask the Father, and he will give you another Counselor to be with you forever—the Spirit of truth. The world cannot accept him, because it neither sees him nor knows him. But you know him, for he lives with you and will be in you.
>
> —John 14:16–17

Jesus told them in verse 26 that this Counselor, this gift, would teach them all things and remind them of everything He had said to them. He went on to tell them in John 16:7 that "unless I go away, the Counselor will not come to you; but if I go, I will send him to you." And when the Holy Spirit comes, Jesus said, "He will guide you into all truth. He will not speak on his own; he will speak only what he hears, and he will tell you what is yet to come" (John 16:13).

Jesus made it clear that the gift of the Holy Spirit is to be with us always and will be so close to us that He will be in us. There is no way we can lose Him or be separated from Him. He will constantly remind us of the truth, the reality of the spirit dimension, and who we are created to be:

> It is written, "No eye has seen, no ear has heard, no mind has conceived what God has prepared for those who love him"—but God has revealed it to us by his Spirit.
> —1 Corinthians 2:9–10

He will also reveal mysteries to us and show us things about the future. God wants us to have a concrete way to know that we are reconnected to Him, that He is with us and we are part of His family. "The Spirit himself testifies with our spirit that we are God's children" (Romans 8:16). He wants us to have a sense of peace and security at all times.

Once we turn from our rebellion and repent and have an encounter with God, we are set free from the spiritual matrix of Satan. The curse of sin and death is reversed in our lives. But we still live in a world polluted by the Fall, surrounded by people who are living in the deception of the spiritual matrix. God knew that we needed more than an encounter with Him to cope with life here. He knew that not only did we need a radical transformation by being born again into the spirit dimension, but we also needed an ongoing presence in our life to keep us there!

That presence is the Holy Spirit.

> We have not received the spirit of the world [the deceptions of the spiritual matrix] but the Spirit who is from God, that we may understand what God has freely given

us.... The [person] without the Spirit [that is, the person in the deception of the spiritual matrix] does not accept the things that come from the Spirit of God, for they are foolishness to him, and he cannot understand them, because they are spiritually discerned.

—1 Corinthians 2:12, 14

You, dear children, are from God and have overcome them [those deceived by the spiritual matrix], because the one who is in you [the Holy Spirit] is greater than the one who is in the world [Satan].

—1 John 4:4

The Holy Spirit is God Himself. As God, He is a person with intellect, will, and emotions. He speaks, listens, comforts, teaches, guides, intercedes, warns, convicts, and loves. As God, He is eternal, all powerful, everywhere present, and all knowing. He is the essence of God Himself. And God wants us not only to have His presence with us but also to be saturated, that is, filled to overflowing, with Him.

A brief note here: if you are keeping count, the Father, the Son Jesus, and the Holy Spirit may sound like three gods, but they are not. There is only one God, just as one times one times one still equals one. I'd like to explain more, but I can't. It is a mystery, which doesn't mean it's a secret God is keeping from us. It's more like a deep spiritual understanding that we are growing into but haven't arrived at yet. Let's face it. If we could understand everything about God, He wouldn't be that big, now would He?

God's Mind Meld

Years ago on television there was a great sci-fi weekly program called *Star Trek*. (Yes, I admit I'm a "Trekkie"!) It was about a starship called the *Enterprise* and its crew, mostly human, who were sent on various missions by an intergalactic federation. One crew member, Mr. Spock, was decidedly not human. He was from the planet Vulcan, which was a race of humanoid beings with pointed ears and computer personalities. He was like a human who was all reason and no emotion. But he had some interesting abilities that humans lacked. He was gifted in decoding communications from alien beings. He would "mind meld" with an alien by placing his head against the alien's head, and he would begin to read his thoughts, feel his feelings, and indeed experience first-hand everything that was going on inside of the alien. For a brief period, Mr. Spock would become one with the alien. This helped the crew understand the aliens and have empathy for them, and in a few cases it alerted them to imminent danger.

When we encounter God, He transforms us through His Spirit of absolute life. He unplugs us from Satan's spiritual matrix and opens up the spirit dimension of His kingdom to us. But He doesn't tamper with our free will. That remains ours to control. He desires intimate relationship with us. He doesn't want us as a distant relative but as a close heart companion. While His Holy Spirit is with us and will never leave us, He wants us to desire intimacy with Him just as He does with us. To use the analogy of Mr. Spock, God longs to mind meld with us. But it's a mind meld in reverse. He is all knowing and knows everything about us. He longs to pour Himself, His Spirit, into us in a way that we will be able to know Him, not just know about Him. He wants to be this close and known by us this much! God doesn't want us left in the dark. He wants to reveal secrets and mysteries to us that are beyond our human perception or ability to know. It is from this position of intimacy with Him that we regain our power and authority of dominion on Earth. Opening up to Him in this way not only reinstates our dominion, but it also begins to have a positive impact on the people and situations around us. We become channels of God's life and power to our world.

We see this invitation being given by Jesus to His followers after His resurrection. He appears to them in a room where they are hiding for fear they might get arrested by the religious leaders. Jesus encourages them and then breathes upon them and tells them: "Receive the Holy Spirit" (John 20:22). In essence He is opening up a God encounter to them and inviting them to enter into their first real spiritual encounter. He is pronouncing that they are transformed and have access to the spirit dimension. He is announcing to them that they are "born again."

But a short time later He says something else to them right before He leaves Earth. He tells them to wait for the promise from the Father God. He tells them they will receive energizing power when the Holy Spirit comes upon them. They will become bold witnesses sharing the good news of the kingdom. And ten days later at the Jewish feast of Pentecost, His followers did receive a powerful infilling of the Holy Spirit. It radically changed them from fearful fugitives hiding from everyone to bold, courageous men who openly proclaimed the good news. They not only talked about the kingdom of God, but they also demonstrated it with power and authority much as Jesus had by healing the sick and performing miracles. Today we refer to this promise as "being baptized in the Spirit" or "being filled with the Spirit." This gift from Father God is as real and available today as it was then, and God's desire is that all His family should seek to receive it.

Footprints of the Holy Spirit

This invitation to intimacy with God is His way of offering Himself to us. All we have to do is desire Him, say yes, and open ourselves to be filled with His Spirit. He will do the rest. This is an activity that takes place in the spirit dimension. But does the Holy Spirit leave any footprints? What changes or signs might we see that let us know the Holy Spirit has filled us? Exact effects differ from person to person, but most people report one or more of the following:

- They have unexplainable peace in stressful situations.

- It is unexpectedly easier for them to keep their cool and not get angry.

- Suddenly the Bible is much easier to understand.

- They may have dreams of spiritual things.

- It is easier to hear God talking to them.

- They sense God's nearness and protection.

- They sense a sudden urgency to pray for a friend or family member.

⊮ They want to spend more time with God and be in His presence.

⊮ They may see visions of the spirit dimension.

⊮ They begin to use a unique prayer language to talk to God.

Sudden urgency to pray

Let me give you examples of a couple of these. I have a friend, Joy Dawson, who is an author and has been a follower of Jesus for many years. She related to me how one day in the middle of an activity she felt a sudden great urgency to pray for a friend of hers who works for a missions group in a foreign country. She said the urgency stayed with her for ten to fifteen minutes, then lifted. Some time later, she was with her friend and mentioned the incident. The two compared notes and discovered that Joy had been prompted to pray for her friend at the exact moment that the plane he was in lost an engine and started into a nose dive. It took ten to fifteen minutes for the pilot to regain control of the plane and insure their safe landing, exactly the time frame in which Joy had felt the urgency to pray.[1] When we are filled with the Holy Spirit, He can partner with us in protecting others, even possibly saving their lives!

The language of the Holy Spirit

I want to mention the subject of a unique prayer language, or speaking in tongues as it is sometimes called. This is a frequent but not universal sign of being filled with the Holy Spirit. Frequently when the Holy Spirit comes upon a person, they will sense a warmth or sometimes an ecstasy and a desire to praise God. When they begin to speak, they find themselves uttering strange words they have never heard before. Usually this is effortless. The words just come as if the mind has been bypassed. When this happens, it is very different from someone talking gibberish that requires a conscious effort on the part of the speaker. Sometimes there is just a phrase repeated over and over. Sometimes there is a flood of words.

This might seem like kind of a strange sign, since you don't know what you are saying. What's the point or value in that? Actually, there's plenty. God knows that when you first encounter Him and reenter the spirit dimension, you have a lot of learning to do. It will take time for you to learn how the spirit dimension operates and how you can take authority there. But He wants you to be able to begin to benefit from your new position with Him from the first day. He wants to give you gifts and resources far past your ability to comprehend. Your mind will have to grow into understanding. So God gives you a secret code that bypasses your mind and allows you to speak mysteries and obtain resources in the spirit dimension that you don't know enough to even ask for but you nonetheless need. In a way, He gives you the ability to speak an alien language, a spiritual one, fluently so you can make progress much more quickly than if you had to learn everything with your mind first. In 1 Corinthians 14:2, the Bible states:

> For anyone who speaks in a tongue does not speak to men but to God. Indeed, no one understands him; he utters mysteries with his spirit.

And again in Jude 20:

But you, dear friends, build yourselves up in your most holy faith and pray in the Holy Spirit [pray in tongues].

How I Met My Best Friend

What is it like to be filled with God the Holy Spirit? Well, just like your first encounter with the divine ET, there is no "one size fits all." God delights, it would seem, in surprising and delighting us. Your experience will be designed by God to perfectly fit who you are and meet your needs. For some people, it is a quiet, peaceful experience where the Holy Spirit enters in a gentle way. One example of this in the Bible is the baptism of Jesus. He was baptized in water, and as He was coming up out of the water, the Holy Spirit descended from heaven upon Him in the form of a dove. A voice came from heaven and said, "This is My Son, whom I love very much. I am very pleased with Him." This story is related by Jesus's cousin, John the Baptist, who baptized Jesus in water. John reports hearing and seeing these things at the time. You can read the full story in Matthew 3:13–17.

On the other hand, when the Holy Spirit filled Jesus's followers, He came in a very dramatic way. Jesus had returned to His Father God in heaven but had told His followers to wait until they received power from on high. They had gathered themselves together, about one hundred twenty of them in a room. They waited for ten days, praying together. They had no time frame, and they didn't know what they were looking for. It didn't matter, because when the Holy Spirit arrived, His entrance was so dramatic that there was no doubt. On the day of the Jewish feast of Pentecost, He swooped in like a huge wind that roared and filled each one of them. And each of them was engulfed in what looked like flames, but this was spiritual, not physical, fire. All of them began speaking fluently in foreign languages they had never heard. The commotion was so great that it attracted a large crowd outside the house they were in. Now that is quite an entrance! (See Acts 2:1–18.)

My own experience I would put somewhere between these two in terms of dramatic intensity. I had become a follower of Jesus in 1973, as I related in the last chapter. That encounter for me was emotionally very intense, and I never doubted its authenticity for a moment. But I had not heard about God's gift of the Holy Spirit. I wanted to know God more deeply, and I wanted to find more friends who also knew Him. Over Easter break in 1974, one of my friends invited me to go on a trip to Niagara Falls with a group of kids from his church. I didn't have any plans for break and liked the idea of a trip and the opportunity to make some new friends.

Niagara Falls was awesome! During the trip we stopped at a couple of churches in the area to attend services. At one church on a Sunday evening, the group I was traveling with gave a mini-concert. We sang several songs that were popular then. One called "Day by Day" was from the musical *Godspell*, and it was one of my favorites. Although I had sung it many times, this particular night I was deeply moved as I sang, and it felt like a prayer coming from deep within me.

> To see Thee more clearly,
> Love Thee more dearly,

Follow Thee more nearly
Day by day.[2]

Somehow it seemed as if the room and all the other people just melted away and God and I were all alone. I was so aware of Him there with me that my heart was bursting: "Yes, God, that is my prayer! Lord, I really mean these words with all my heart. I'm not just singing them. God, I really want to see You more clearly. I really want to love You more dearly. And God, I really want to follow You more nearly, day by day."

As I began to worship God, His presence intensified, and I felt tears running down my face. I began to feel a tingling, electrifying sensation in my feet, which quickly traveled up my legs, up to my head, through my arms, and down to my fingers. The sensation became so intense that I could not move my fingers. I tried to make a fist, but I could not. I felt too wonderful to be frightened! The tingling became a pulsing sensation, and I began to sob with joy. I knew it was God, and I knew He was touching me in a way I had never heard of or experienced before. I began shaking and sobbing uncontrollably.

I certainly hadn't anticipated anything like this on my trip to Niagara Falls. I wanted to make friends and see the falls, and now I felt as though I were Niagara Falls! Our group leader came over and politely asked me to leave the room. I literally had to force my body to leave, but I did manage to make it to the men's room. I continued to weep and worship. I knew God was touching me for a reason. I did not hear an audible voice or see anything, but I knew in my heart that God had heard my prayer of dedication and service. I knew this touch was a touch of power. I knew this power was being given to me to give service to Him. I now know it was the first (although not the last) time I was filled with the Holy Spirit. Over the years I have come to value His presence with me like no other. He counsels, guides, comforts, instructs, warns, and laughs with me. I trust His love for me totally. He is truly my best friend.

It's Your Turn

The first time we receive this wonderful gift of the Holy Spirit is often very memorable. But God does not want it to be an isolated experience. He knows that we need continual infilling of the Holy Spirit to remain strong and full of spiritual wisdom and power. Just as we need to refuel our bodies daily by taking in fresh food and water, we need to refuel our spirits by continually being filled with the Holy Spirit. The apostle Paul, a follower of Jesus, wrote: "Do not be drunk with wine....Instead be filled with the [Holy] Spirit" (Ephesians 5:18). The Holy Spirit will take you much higher than alcohol ever could anyway. The Holy Spirit will open life to you in a whole new dimension, so you learn how to walk and live in the spirit realm, not just occasionally glimpse it. I've made it a habit to ask for a fresh infilling every morning.

You may have had your first encounter with God at the end of the previous chapter just minutes ago. Or you may have encountered God years ago, but you never realized He had another gift for you. It makes no difference. God is always eager to gift His children who are ready and willing to receive what He has for them. Would you like to receive the infilling of the Holy Spirit now? All you have to do is ask and believe He desires to fill you. Be open to how the Holy Spirit comes to you. If you feel like praying or praising Him, go for it. And don't be surprised if you receive a heavenly language. Many people do. If you do, use it often. Speaking in tongues will strengthen your spirit. Most of all, enjoy the gift of the Holy Spirit! He is your personal forever companion and friend. And He will guide and accompany you on the most exciting adventure you have ever known: your destiny in God.

Just like your initial encounter with God, there are no magic words or one right way to receive the infilling of the Holy Spirit. Some people ask others who are followers of Jesus to pray with them or put hands on them and pray to receive the infilling. With others or alone, you simply need to let God know you love Him, you want to follow Him, and you are ready to receive His gift of the Holy Spirit. For those of you who feel more comfortable with a guide, I offer the following prayer. Remember, just like your initial encounter with God, it is the sincere desire of your heart, not the eloquence of your words, that is important to God.

Dear Father God, I come to You in the wonderful name of Jesus. I acknowledge that I have rebelled and gone my own way. But I have repented of my rebellion and accepted Your invitation to encounter You and live in the spirit dimension. I now give up my own way and acknowledge that I want to follow You all the days of my life. I surrender all my former control to You. Father God, I believe that You desire to give me the gift of Your Holy Spirit. I ask You right now to fill me with

Your Holy Spirit. Grant me the power of the Holy Spirit
to do Your work in His power and to find my destiny
in You. Thank You, Father God, for Your love and Your
gift of the Holy Spirit to me. Amen.

No matter what happens or what doesn't, what you feel or what you don't, praise God for His gift to you. You have asked, and you have received. You will see differences. The footprints of the Holy Spirit will be unmistakable. You can count on it. Now that you have encountered God and been empowered with His gift of the Holy Spirit, you are prepared to boldly go where you have never been: your destiny in Him!

⤜(10)⤛

TO BOLDLY GO
WHERE YOU HAVE
NEVER BEEN BEFORE

I've already admitted to being a "Trekkie" as a child. One of my favorite parts of each *Star Trek* episode was the very beginning when Captain Kirk would give the date from the captain's log and repeat the mission of the starship *Enterprise*. It was "to explore strange new worlds. To seek out new life and new civilizations. To boldly go where no man has gone before."[1] At that pronouncement my pulse would rev up and my curiosity would kick in. I couldn't wait to see where we would be going and what adventures the crew and I would encounter in that episode. I could imagine myself as part of the *Enterprise* crew, boldly moving into space at warp speed, looking at worlds and creatures human eyes had never seen before. It all seemed so potentially real even though it was a television program. And deep within me something stirred at the thought of one day actually journeying into unchartered territory somewhere "out there." It seemed somehow like I was born for it. It was my destiny.

Perhaps you can relate to this inner sense, if not about space travel, then about some other type of exploits you dreamed of as a child. I think all of us carry dreams within—dreams of significance, dreams of purpose, dreams of fulfilling some destiny that will give our life meaning. I know this not only from my own life experience but also from talking to countless others over many years interacting with people of all ages and racial, ethnic, and cultural groups. Not too long ago, a book entitled *The Purpose-Driven Life* became a runaway best seller in the United States. I think people want purpose in their lives, to indeed know that their life must have some purpose. That inner desire made the book a literary hit.

Your Destiny in God

I believe the divine ET is a being of purpose and destiny and that He created each one of us to have our own unique purpose and destiny. Our existence here has meaning. There is a course to run, a mission to complete. Each of us is an original, born with unique attributes, characteristics, and abilities that complement each other and equip us to fill a unique purpose here on Earth. You may have heard the saying or read the bumper sticker slogan, "God doesn't make junk." It's true; God doesn't make anything that is redundant or worthless, and He doesn't make anything that is pointless either. Your very existence means that you bear the imprint of your Creator, God Himself, for you are created in His image. To discount or disrespect you, He would have to discount or disrespect Himself.

On the contrary, you are so valuable and irreplaceable to God that He wants to partner with you to discover your identity and purpose. If you have said yes to an encounter with the divine ET, you have just embarked on your greatest adventure in life: discovering your destiny in God, for that is where your identity and purpose are located. In Colossians 3:3, the apostle Paul stated, "Your [new, real] life is hidden with Christ *[Jesus]* in God" (AMP). God wants to see you fulfilled. He wants your life to be happy and productive. He wants you to respect yourself and to enjoy your accomplishments. Jesus told us His purpose in becoming human and coming to Earth, making Himself known to us: "I have come that they [that means you!] may have life, and have it to the full" (John 10:10). He was talking about giving us absolute life and all the fulfillment that goes with it. In Ephesians 3:20 the Bible tells us that God is able and willing to do far more for us than anything we could ever think or even imagine. He wants our life to be so complete and satisfying.

We read in Jeremiah 29:11:

"For I know the plans I have for you," declares the LORD, "plans to prosper you and not to harm you, plans to give you hope and a future."

And this theme is repeated in Ephesians 2:10:

For we are God's workmanship, created in Christ Jesus to do good works, which God prepared in advance for us to do.

God has a purpose and destiny designed just for you. Does this mean that He wants to force-fit you into some design He has? Never! Remember, first and foremost, God is loving, so loving in fact that He is love itself. He will never force or coerce you to do or be anything. But being the Creator and sustainer of the universe (that is, everything that is), He does know a few things, even about us, that we don't. He desires daily companionship with you. He wants to reveal secrets to you about yourself. He is all knowing and would like to share His wisdom and insight with you. You will always have freedom to do what you choose, but He hopes over time that as the two of you walk in friendship together, you will come to trust in Him and believe that He desires your deepest happiness. Your discovery of your identity and purpose will be yours, but He wants to partner with you on your journey.

Your Destiny Voyage

When I was watching *Star Trek*, I liked to imagine what it would be like to come aboard ship the first time. I could see myself in the hallways, down in the engine room with Scotty, at the infirmary with Bones, the ship's doctor, and on the bridge with Captain Kirk and Lieutenant Spock. I could see myself talking with them, getting on-the-job training under their guidance. I could also see myself in my assigned quarters, reading the ship's operation manuals. I knew I would have to "learn the ship" and communicate with the other crew members. It would take time to develop familiarity with the ship's operating procedures and feel confident that I knew the responsibilities of my position. I would not be able to penetrate deep, undiscovered realms of space on my own. It would take the combined effort of each crew member to complete a successful mission and fulfill our stated purpose.

A space exploration takes ongoing communication, in-depth instruction, and the coordinated efforts of an entire crew. Your personal destiny voyage is no different. It is not something you can complete or accomplish entirely on your own, isolated from the knowledge and support of others. First and foremost, of course, are the instruction and communication you will receive from the divine ET Himself, but you also need the insight, help, and encouragement of others who, like you, are on their destiny voyage. As you begin to boldly go where you have never been before, I want to tell you about some important ways you can gain more insight and skill in your pursuit of your destiny voyage.

"E.T. Phone Home"

Do you remember the movie *E.T. the Extra-Terrestrial*?[2] E.T. was a cute little alien creature who was left behind on Earth when his fellow aliens had to leave suddenly to avoid detection. He was eventually befriended by three children determined to somehow help him reconnect with his own kind and to be able to return home. There is a scene where E.T. points to the sky and states to one of the children, "E.T. phone home," meaning that he was lonely and wanting to communicate with home. As you begin your destiny voyage with God, it is important to "phone home" often, that is, stay in daily communication with the divine ET. Getting to know God is no different than getting to know anyone else you want to know. How do you get to know someone in whom you are interested? You must spend time with them. You must communicate what you think, what you feel, what you like, what you dislike, and so on, and so must they. You must each share, and you must each listen. When you want to get to know someone, this isn't hard to do. In fact, you want to do it, and you find it enjoyable.

God wants to hear your concerns, thoughts, dreams, and desires. He wants to share His thoughts, plans, purposes, and desires with you. He desires this intimate exchange with you every day. And it's easy to do. It is called prayer. Does that surprise you? If so, it may be because there are many misunderstandings about prayer. You may think of it as a religious activity that can only be done in certain places like church or in certain ways like on your knees or with your hands folded and head bowed. You may think prayer can only be said in certain ways like reading prayers at a religious service or saying the Lord's Prayer. Nothing could be further from reality. The truth is, there is no "right" way to pray. And the words aren't that important. It's the sincerity and desires of your heart that matter most to God.

Once you invite the divine ET to encounter you, you can communicate with Him at any time, at any place, and in any activity by simply talking to Him. You may talk aloud, or you may talk through your thoughts to Him. He can receive both types of communication with equal ease. You will find that His line is never busy, nor will you ever get connected to a divine voice-mail system. He is always available, always listening, and always joyful to hear your voice. You may never have thought of prayer as communication with God, but that is exactly what it is.

Be assured that as you pray daily, you will find your own way and words that work best for you and God. The more you communicate with God, the better you will know Him and the more comfortable you will be in talking to Him. However, I can offer you some general guidelines for prayer that will help you get started.

Prayer is dialogue.

All good communication involves both talking and listening. We talk to reveal ourselves to another, to be known, and to hopefully be accepted and valued. We listen to understand and hopefully to increase our caring and empathy for each other. Both are necessary if true communication exists. And quite frankly, where most of us have difficulty is on the listening end. We all like to talk and be heard, but it is harder to be still and hear the heart of the other person. Listening is as important in prayer as it is in talking. Otherwise we will treat God like a cosmic bellhop who is supposed to listen to all our thoughts and concerns and do what we think should be done. We never give Him the opportunity to respond and share His insight with us, which might cause us to view the situation in a whole different way. I'm sure you have had the experience of being on the mute end with someone who just wanted to talk at you but really didn't want any input. You probably felt frustrated and just hoped they would stop talking—and soon! You didn't feel as if you were being valued in the conversation, and you probably didn't like the experience. We need to remember that God wants to communicate with us, which means that in addition to listening to us, He talks and we listen.

But what does it sound like when God talks? Don't expect to hear an audible voice talking to you. While that can and has happened to some people in isolated situations, it is not the norm. Most likely you will have an inner sense or urging that will prompt you to take a particular course of action. It may be an action related to a minor event; for example, just getting a sense to "turn down here" at a crowded mall parking lot. And just when you do, someone pulls out, leaving you a space. Yes, believe it or not, God likes to help with events as mundane as finding a parking space.

But becoming sensitive to the urgings of God's Spirit can also have important consequences. I remember attending a church-sponsored conference a number of years ago. Several conference participants came in late, but they had quite an experience to relate. As they were driving to the conference, it was getting dark, and they were on a mountainous road. As they were going up a steep hill with a sharp turn to the left, the driver recalled that he felt a strong urging to pull over into a turnout space at the crest of the curve. Initially he ignored the urging, but it rapidly intensified, and, at the last moment, he pulled to the side. His passengers were confused and began asking him, "What's wrong? Why did you stop?" He had no real explanation except for his inner sense of urgency.

As he was beginning to explain to his traveling companions, another car rushed past them and rounded the corner. A few seconds later they heard a loud crash. They immediately exited their car and ran around the corner. There they saw a semitruck jackknifed across the road. The other car had no opportunity to avoid hitting it broadside, and the driver and his passengers were seriously injured. After summoning help and filling out a police report, the conference participants resumed their journey. The driver was thanking God for warning him of the danger on the road, but he was troubled. He related asking God, "Why didn't you warn the people in the other car?" And he heard God reply quietly, "I did, but they weren't listening."

Learn how to listen for God's voice. In the Bible God says, "Be still, and know that I am God" (Psalm 46:10). When you pray, don't do all the talking. Get quiet, and be still. Expect God to communicate back to you. It may be through an inner urging like described above. It may be a still, small, inner voice that sounds very much like your own, but you know it isn't you. The more you practice listening and following what you hear, the easier it will become to accurately hear God. Communicating with God is like communicating with anyone else. The more time you spend with Him talking and listening, the more familiar you will become with the ways He talks to you.

Prayer is appreciation.

Think of someone you know who is a good friend, someone you really enjoy being with. Your friend probably points out what you are good at and then compliments you on your strengths and achievements. When you have a success, that friend is ready to celebrate it with you. Friends like this let you know when you have helped them by thanking you. It feels good to be around them. They don't complain to you or criticize you all the time. God wants to have this type of communication with you. He wants to hear about your successes and share in celebrating with you. He wants to help you discover your abilities and grow in your confidence in using them. Some people have a hard time believing this, but God wants to tell you good things about yourself. He wants to encourage you and build you up. Unfortunately, some people are convinced that God only talks to you to point out your mistakes and flaws, to "put you in your place." They haven't spent much time talking with God, or they would know that this is not the case.

God likes to hear what He has done right, too. Does that surprise you? When God helps you, He likes to be thanked. He enjoys it when you tell Him what you appreciate about His character and His presence in your life. In prayer this is called thanksgiving and praise. And the Bible tells us to thank and praise God often: "Enter his gates with thanksgiving and his courts with praise. Give thanks to him and praise his name" (Psalm 100:4). "Praise the LORD. Give thanks to the LORD, for he is good; his love endures forever" (Psalm 106:1). You are not encouraged to do this because God needs you to build up His self-esteem. God is not an egomaniac. He doesn't need to always be the center of your attention. Rather, God is a lover, and He desires intimacy with you. He knows that when you spend time focusing on the ways He is good to you, you will grow in trust with Him. As you do, you will open up more to Him and let Him do more for and with you. The Bible describes it this way: the Lord dwells in the praises of His people. (See Psalm 22:3, AMP.) The more we thank and praise Him, the more we focus on His goodness to us, and the more trusting and comfortable we are in His presence. We become more open and intimate with Him.

If you think for a minute, this same principle of appreciation works in all your relationships. When people give you genuine praise and thank you for what you do, you want to stick around them and do more with and for them. When you praise and thank them for what they do for you, you feel more open and warm to them. You want to get to know them more, and your trust in relating to them grows. Our relationship with God works the same way.

Prayer is sharing concerns.

Casual acquaintances will listen to happy things, but true friends care about your pain, disappointment, and sadness, too. They are there in good times and in bad. They don't desert you just because you are going through a hard time. In fact, they want to hear your struggles, and to the extent they are able, they want to help. God is the best friend you will ever have. He wants you to share all your concerns and struggles with Him, no matter how large or small. He wants to comfort and care for you, and He wants to help you in practical, concrete ways as well. The apostle Peter told us, "Cast all your anxiety on him because he cares for you" (1 Peter 5:7). Jesus Himself gave us this reassurance:

Come to me, all you who are weary and burdened, and I will give you rest. Take my yoke upon you and learn from me, for I am gentle and humble in heart, and you will find rest for your souls. For my yoke is easy and my burden is light.

—Matthew 11:28–30

What did Jesus mean by these words? I think He wants you to understand that He not only wants to hear about your concerns, but He also wants you to give them to Him. He will show you a way through your problems. He wants to shoulder your cares and in exchange give you rest and peace. He wants you to be free from anxiety and worry. He wants you to trust Him to provide solutions to problems and comfort for pain and sadness. God promises in Joshua 1:5: "I will be with you; I will never leave you nor forsake you." He is not a fair-weather friend. He is a friend that will never turn on you, never become tired or disappointed with you, never get overwhelmed with your struggles. He is a forever friend.

God wants you to trust Him and believe that He will help you as He has promised. Jesus commented that humans, even though they are fallen and are imperfect, love and want to take good care of their children. He reminded us that if our children ask for bread (something to eat), we don't give them a stone. We give them food. If we know how to give good things to our children when they ask us, don't we know that God will give us good things when we ask Him? He said, "If you…know how to give good gifts to your children, how much more will your Father in heaven give good gifts to those who ask him!" (Matthew 7:11). The apostle Paul reminds us, "My God will meet all your needs according to his glorious riches in Christ Jesus" (Philippians 4:19). The apostle John stated, "This is the confidence we have in approaching God: that if we ask anything according to his will, he hears us. And if we know that he hears us—whatever we ask—we know that we have what we asked of him" (1 John 5:14–15).

God wants to provide for you. He is always ready to hear your concerns and show you the way through your situation. But you have to trust His willingness and believe He will provide. You demonstrate your trust by listening to His guidance and doing what He says to you. You must learn to hear what God is saying to you, believe it is the truth and that it will happen, and act on it. This is called faith, and without it you cannot get to first base in the spirit dimension. You will find as you journey with God that if you develop the habit of listening, believing, and doing, your trust and confidence in God's provision for you will grow and grow.

So far I've focused on God listening to your concerns, but you do remember that prayer is dialogue, right? God wants to share His concerns with you. Not all of them, of course. He is running the universe, so that would be overwhelming! But He does trust you, and He wants to share some of His concerns with you. For example, He might bring a friend to mind and urge you to call that person. When you do, you may find that your friend is in a hard place and so appreciates an encouraging call or maybe having you come over and hang out for a while. Someone you know might be sharing a concern with you, and God may encourage you to pray with him or her. This might be hard if you have never done it before, but offer to do so anyway. I have offered to pray with many people when they were stressed out about something, and I have almost never had them say, "No thanks." In fact, almost always they are so thankful and know that I really care about what is happening to them.

I find that most of the time God shares His concerns with me by prompting me to help or call or just spend time with someone, usually someone I know. You see, God cares for all of us, and He knows just what will be the most helpful to each of us and when. If we remain open and let God share His concerns with us and follow His prompts, we will be able to help and encourage others when they need it most.

Prayer is a clean slate.

All of us have experienced having a falling-out or misunderstanding with a friend. As long as we avoided each other, the hard feelings remained and often grew with the mutual silence. But when we got together and talked about what went wrong, even if we were hurt or angry at first, we were able to find a way to get past our difficulty and reestablish our relating again. I hope you have had this experience of reconciling with a friend after a problem has occurred. It is a wonderful feeling, and often the friendship is stronger for having weathered a hard time without breaking apart. We rediscover our friendship, and the repaired relationship is like getting back a wonderful gift we temporarily lost.

We do not have falling-outs with God, and He does not get angry and refuse to relate to us. But because we retain our free will and the right to choose, we will sometimes still choose to go our own way and do our own thing. When we do, we part company with God and put distance between Him and ourselves. This doesn't destroy our relationship, but it interferes with our intimacy with Him. It breaks down our communication. Our natural tendency when this happens is to avoid God, the same way we avoid an offended friend. But this only prolongs our lack of contact and delays the repair of our communication with Him. When you sin (rebel and do your own thing), don't run away from God as Adam and Eve did in the garden. Instead, run to God and simply own up to what you've done. Be courageous. Be honest. Be transparent. The moment you confess, God forgives you, and your intimacy is restored. God will not harass you or keep reminding you of your failure. He will not try to make you feel worthless or guilty. He loves you and wants open dialogue with you. He wants the channels of communication to stay open between you. Talking to Him about your slips, your faults, and your mistakes is the way you keep the slate clean and preserve the closeness of your friendship with God. And the more you are honest with yourself and Him in this way, the more confident you will become about His love for you.

Pray in the Spirit.

If you received a heavenly prayer language when you asked God to fill you with the Holy Spirit, use it! If you have yet to receive this gift, keep asking God for it and expect to get it! The Holy Spirit knows how to pray more perfectly than we do, for He is intimately acquainted with the spirit dimension, while we are only learning. He is always willing to give you counsel and guidance about what and how to pray. And He will pray beyond your thoughts and dreams if you allow Him to.

> "No eye has seen, no ear has heard, no mind has conceived what God has prepared for those who love him"—but

God has revealed it to us by his [Holy] Spirit. The [Holy] Spirit searches all things, even the deep things of God.

—1 Corinthians 2:9–10

No one knows the thoughts of God except the [Holy] Spirit of God.

—1 Corinthians 2:11

This is what we speak, not in words taught by human wisdom but in words taught by the [Holy] Spirit, expressing spiritual truth in spiritual words.

—1 Corinthians 2:13

The apostle Paul wanted us to understand how important the help of the Holy Spirit is in our prayers. He said:

The [Holy] Spirit helps us in our weakness. We do not know what we ought to pray for, but the [Holy] Spirit himself intercedes for us with groans that words cannot express. And he who searches our hearts knows the mind of the [Holy] Spirit, because the [Holy] Spirit intercedes for the saints in accordance with God's will.

—Romans 8:26–27

Make it your goal to learn how to let the Holy Spirit guide your prayers. Pray in your heavenly language frequently, and be assured that you are speaking spiritual mysteries that are light-years beyond where your mind can currently take you. You can move into spiritual depths in your communication with God even though you have only known Him a short time. He wants it that way. He is inviting you to become intimately acquainted with Him and to allow Him to partner with you on your destiny voyage. Prayer or talking with God is essential to moving ahead in the spirit dimension. In the next chapter we will look at another activity that opens up kingdom living and helps you pursue your destiny in God.

⑪

THE USER'S MANUAL
FOR ANOTHER REALITY

In the movie *The Matrix*, Neo makes the decision to enter the world of reality outside the Matrix. He has to be unplugged from the Matrix and deprogrammed. This is a challenging process and a lot more than Neo could anticipate, as his entire understanding of reality undergoes a profound metamorphosis. If you remember, his body goes through a rigorous deprogramming process that takes significant time. When he comes to consciousness at the end of the process, he is weak and somewhat disoriented. Morpheus, the resistance leader, tells Neo, "Your muscles have atrophied. We will rebuild them." Neo is blinking in the bright light and asks, "Why do my eyes hurt?" Morpheus replies, "You've never used them before."[1]

Later, when Neo has regained some strength, Morpheus introduces him to the reprogramming process. The Matrix has been taken out of him, but if Neo is to survive and thrive in the world of reality outside the Matrix, he must understand how that reality operates and his destiny in it. Morpheus informs Neo that he now has an implantation device for his mind at the base of his skull. It is through this mind implant that he will learn the ways of the new world of reality in which he is now living. In the movie, the resistance fighters are able to download any type of mental projection into Neo's mind and give him instructions on new skills and abilities that he can exercise outside the confines of the Matrix. The first thing we see is Neo learning martial arts maneuvers, and we watch as he improves with practice.

Initially Neo protests to Morpheus that the mental projections are not real. This way of learning and experiencing reality is foreign to Neo's experience up to this point. Morpheus replies, "What is *real*? How do you define *real*? If you're talking about what you can feel . . . smell . . . taste and see, then *real* is simply electrical signals interpreted by your brain."[2] Over time Neo comes to trust the reality of the download process more and more. He understands that his trust in this process can actually allow him to reenter and leave the actual Matrix without becoming reabsorbed in its reality. He can see and understand the reality of the Matrix and his former life there, but he is now living in a larger reality outside the confines of the Matrix. He begins to understand that part of his destiny is helping others deprogram from the Matrix and enter the world of reality outside it.

Downloads of Another Reality

Just as Neo needed to understand the operations of the world of reality outside the Matrix and discover his new destiny, you need to learn the operations of the reality of the spirit dimension. You begin by strengthening your familiarity with spiritual reality, largely by learning to "see" with your spiritual eyes. In the physical dimension we are used to using our physical eyes to see objects and people. But we know even in the physical dimension that just because we can't see something doesn't mean it is not real or doesn't exist. For example, we can't "see" electricity or atoms, but we know they exist anyway. In the world of spirit reality, you must learn to use the spiritual sense of faith to understand and experience spiritual things. The more you exercise faith, the deeper your awareness of the spirit dimension becomes, and the more you experience your spiritual skills and abilities. Just like with Neo, it takes repeated exposure and practice. It also involves the progressive transformation of your mind. You begin to learn how to tune in your mind to spiritual reality as well as physical reality. As you do, you increasingly enter the spirit dimension and discover your destiny there.

Neo had an implantation device in his skull through which he could receive mental projection downloads. How will you receive downloads from the spirit dimension? The divine ET has supplied a user's manual for the spirit dimension. It is a codebook that remains locked to those living in Satan's spiritual matrix, as they are trapped in the physical dimension. But once you have an encounter with the divine ET and surrender doing life your way, you begin to enter another reality, the spiritual one. And the codebook will begin to open to you. That codebook is the Bible.

In the first chapter of this book I introduced the Bible to you as a true communication from the divine ET. It is actually a compilation of books written over a period of two thousand years, and yet it forms an integrated whole. The Bible contains an account of God's interest in the human race and His ongoing relationship with us. It describes His original intentions and plans for us to have dominion here on Earth in preparation for coreigning with Him in the heavens. It chronicles our disastrous decision to go our own way and depart from our relationship with Him. However, even though we fell out of our place in the spirit dimension into the physical dimension, He did not abandon us. The Bible tells us He loved us so much that He became one of us; He came to Earth and lived among us, demonstrating the reality of the spirit dimension. He died, blew hell wide apart, and came back from death to extend an invitation to us to reenter His kingdom and regain our original dominion and destiny in Him. And He sent the Holy Spirit to be our guide, friend, and counselor to instruct us on how to develop our spiritual skills and abilities. The Bible opens up all these events to us. In one way it can be described as a cosmic love letter to the human race from the divine ET.

As you become increasingly familiar with the Bible, you will find that it contains several powerful and repetitive themes. These themes are foundational for God, and He did not want us to miss them. They are His constant love for us, His reaching out to us even when we were in total rebellion, and His never-ending desire for reconciliation and restoration with His human family. God is not trying to hide anything from you. He wants to reveal His heart to you and help you reenter the spirit dimension you were created to live and have dominion in. As you spend time in the Bible, He downloads spiritual reality to you.

Meet the Alien Author

While the Bible was penned over many years by different authors, there was a divine force directing and guiding the entire two-thousand-year project. That divine force is the Holy Spirit. The Holy Spirit moved on people and impelled them to write, but the inspiration for the content came through the Spirit.

> For no prophecy *[or scripture]* ever originated because some man willed it [to do so—it never came by human impulse], but men spoke from God who were borne along (moved and impelled) by the Holy Spirit.
> —2 Peter 1:21, AMP

Once you encounter the divine ET, you receive the Holy Spirit. You do not need a mental implantation device in your skull as Neo did to learn about the new reality you have entered. You have something much better. You have a transformational presence, the Holy Spirit of God living with and in you. The author of the codebook is as near to you as your next breath, and He provides you with divine insight and understanding.

The anointing [Holy Spirit] you received from him [Jesus] remains in you, and you do not need for anyone to teach you. But as his [Jesus's] anointing [Holy Spirit] teaches you about all things and as that anointing is real, not counterfeit—just as it [the Holy Spirit] has taught you, remain in him [Jesus].

—1 John 2:27

This does not mean that it is not helpful to listen to the teaching of others on Bible content. But it does mean that the Holy Spirit is your own personal mentor who will help you receive and understand downloads from the Bible about living in the spirit dimension.

What is a download from the Bible like? What happens when the Holy Spirit guides and instructs you? The first thing you need to know about the Bible is that through the action of the Holy Spirit, it is alive and will interact with you. What am I saying? Let me explain with an example. I have a friend who recently related to me the memory of her first Bible download from the spirit realm. She was sixteen at the time and at a summer camp. She had read parts of the Bible before but found it hard to understand. She had been assigned to read 2 Timothy, so she was plodding through it. She got to the second chapter and verse 20 when something very different happened.

She described it like this:

I was lying on the bunk reading, when suddenly it felt like my body was lightly tingling all over. I felt so alive, like some type of energy field was surrounding me. Everything around me faded and seemed far away. I began reading verses 20 and 21. As I did, it felt like blinders were falling off my eyes and I "saw" something "spiritual" for the first time. It wasn't a physical seeing but an internal one. It felt like someone turned on a huge brilliant light in my mind and was talking softly, directly to me. Immediately I knew what the verses meant and that God was talking to me through those words. He was letting me know that I would determine what the meaning and quality of my life would be. He was inviting me to a high life with Him. It was so clear.

Here are the verses that were downloaded to her:

But in a great house there are not only vessels of gold and silver, but also [utensils] of wood and earthenware, and some for honorable and noble [use] and some for menial...[use]. So whoever cleanses himself...[and] [separates himself from contaminating and corrupting influences] will [then himself] be...set apart...for honorable and noble purposes...and profitable to the Master...ready for any good work.
—2 Timothy 2:20–21, AMP

She explained:

I knew God was making it clear that we carry the deciding vote about the significance of our lives. We can surrender our way and attain a life that is like a silver or gold vessel. It has great worth and meaning. Or if we choose, we can insist on doing our own thing, waste our life away, and end up a little mud pot with nothing special to show we were here. It is our choice. God wants us to know that greatness and quality of life are possible for any one of us.

In reading the Bible, my friend had a powerful firsthand encounter with the alien author—the Holy Spirit. She shared with me that the experience made her so aware of the spirit dimension that she wanted to receive more downloads. She began reading the Bible regularly and expecting downloads to occur, and they did.

Warning: This User's Manual Is Not for Wimps

How can a book written so long ago speak so strongly and be so relevant today? Why has it survived centuries of use and outlived culture after culture? What about it has challenged people to sacrifice their lives to obtain it? Let me share with you several specific qualities that make the Bible a timeless manual that contains user instructions for living in the spirit dimension—the kingdom of God.

Truth versus knowledge

While the Bible contains factual information, it is not focused on knowledge but on truth. Knowledge can change with additional scientific inquiry. We all now know that the universe is vast and expanding at a phenomenal rate. But as I mentioned in chapter 1, less than one hundred years ago, it was generally accepted "knowledge" that what we now call the Milky Way galaxy was the entire universe and was believed to be held in a static state by opposing gravitational forces. A powerful telescope changed our thinking radically. Knowledge can be influenced by scientific discovery, new technology, culture, gender, race, and even by political correctness. But truth is timeless. It does not change. It is true in every culture, every racial group, and every political system. The Bible is a book of truth. It addresses head-on the tough, timeless questions of truth, such as: "Who am I?" "Why am I here?" "What is life about?"

Strengthen the sense of faith

Faith is the sense of the spirit dimension. It is the way you contact and connect with the spiritual realm. You can know spiritual reality through faith as strongly as you know physical reality through your five senses. You develop faith by hearing God's Word. "Faith comes by hearing, and hearing by the word of God" (Romans 10:17, NKJV). The more time you spend reading the Bible and letting the Holy Spirit instruct and guide you, the stronger and deeper your faith will become. Faith involves listening to God's Word, believing God's Word, and acting on God's Word. Trust in God grows as we pay attention to what He says, do it, and see the results. We learn by experience that if we will hear and obey, our trust and confidence in Him will grow.

Interactive experience

The Bible is a living document, not a piece of literature. You may enjoy a book and reread a section you particularly like. While you may see something new in the way the author wrote the words, you will get the same meaning the tenth time as you did the first. The Bible is different. The Bible speaks to you. No matter how many times you reread a particular section, it will continue to show you new aspects of the spirit dimension. When you read the Bible, you open your spirit to hear God's words from His Holy Spirit. He wants to open the operations of His spirit kingdom to you. He wants to share His intentions with you.

> Every Scripture is God-breathed (given by His inspiration) and is profitable for instruction . . . (in holy living, in conformity to God's will in thought, purpose, and action).
> —2 Timothy 3:16, AMP

Self-revelation

You not only read the Bible. The Bible is the only book that "reads" you. The Bible will reveal you to yourself. This may not always be comfortable, but it is the only way to progress in the spirit dimension. You cannot develop your spiritual skills and abilities fully until you understand your strengths and have dealt with your weaknesses. Hebrews 4:12 describes God's Word this way:

> For the word of God is living and active. Sharper than any double-edged sword, it penetrates even to dividing soul and spirit, joints and marrow; it judges the thoughts and attitudes of the heart.

Ouch! That is deep and unrelenting self-revelation! No charades. No social personas. No clever excuses. No blame shifting. The Bible reveals us as we truly are to ourselves. It is not a manual for the fainthearted. It is not a place for wimps to hide. But it does promise that if we are courageous enough to look into the mirror of self-reflection it holds up to us, the Bible will provide us with instruction to overcome our weaknesses. It will show us how to become strong in the spirit dimension and able to use our dominion and authority to bring positive change into our lives.

Energizing power

God's words are not carriers of thoughts and ideas. They are vehicles of power and change. God's words believed, spoken, and acted upon change circumstances in the physical dimension. God Himself says, "My word…goes out from my mouth: it will not return to me empty, but will accomplish what I desire and achieve the purpose for which I sent it" (Isaiah 55:11). God created us to have this same spirit power, but to attain it we must become highly familiar with the operations of the spirit dimension. We must understand what God's words mean and get to know Him well enough that we believe what He says. God wants us to be change agents. He wants us to walk in power and authority and use His words to overcome the curse of sin and death here on Earth. The only way we can do this is to become familiar with what He says in the Bible. It helps to memorize verses that speak strongly to you. The more we put His Word inside us, the more it transforms our thinking and the stronger we become in spirit power.

Destiny revelation

You have an identity and a destiny in the spirit dimension. It is hidden in Christ Jesus in your relationship with Father God. As you come to know God better, you unwrap and reveal your own destiny. Spending time in the Bible is an important way to learn more about God and become more intimate with Him. The Bible will provide you with insight and clarification. It will show you the way. Psalm 119:105 states, "Your word is a lamp to my feet and a light for my path."

How to Get REAl

I could describe other qualities of the Bible. It is truly a book like no other, a book of incredible transforming power. However, it will only transform you to the extent that you spend time in it. The Bible is a portal to another reality, the spirit dimension. You need to walk through that portal on a daily basis. To stay connected to the spirit dimension, you need to get REAL. Here is how.

Read

The Bible is not just a book. It is an interactive experience. When you read the Bible you ingest spiritual life that nourishes your spirit and causes it to grow, the same way food nourishes your physical body. You must eat frequently every day to keep your body performing optimally. And you must feed your spirit daily to keep yourself connected and in tune with the spirit realm. It helps to establish a pattern so you will be sure to make time each day to read the Bible. For me, personally, I find that spending time each morning before I begin my other activities helps me to refocus on spiritual reality. It establishes an orientation I take with me the whole day. I am more focused and clarified, and things go smoother. On days when I get caught up in activity and my time in the Bible is disrupted, I run around scattered like a chicken with my head cut off, and nothing seems to come together well.

There are so many wonderful people in the Bible through whom you can learn spiritual truths. But I would like to suggest that you go to the source Himself. Jesus is the clearest and truest example of spiritual truth, for He is God in human flesh. A good place to begin reading the Bible is to look at the life, the words, and actions of Jesus. These are recorded in the first four books in the New Testament: Matthew, Mark, Luke, and John, which are called the Gospels, which means "good news." Establish a regular time for Bible reading and stick to it, just like an athlete on a training schedule. Regular spiritual workouts each day will build your spiritual power much more effectively than marathon sessions once a week.

Expect

Remember that the Holy Spirit is your instructor, guide, and counselor. Before you read, invite the Holy Spirit to give you a personal download of spiritual truth. Ask Him to reveal something for you this day. Read and reflect. Be quiet, pray, stay open, and expect that the Holy Spirit will communicate with you. Some people find it helpful to jot down what the Spirit shows them. Or if a particular verse jumps out at you, you may want to write it down and memorize it. Allow the Holy Spirit to communicate with you in different ways. One day it may be a phrase, another time a verse, and still another time you may see yourself as one of the characters in a scene. Sometimes the Spirit will speak to you about yourself, your circumstances, or your concerns. Other times the Spirit may use the Bible reading to make you more aware of the life circumstances of someone else. Sometimes He will point out particular instructions for daily living. At other times He may simply come and surround you with the warm energy of His presence like a hug. And every once in a while you may feel like you hit a wall and nothing happens. Don't quit. Be like the seasoned runner who keeps on regardless. You will break through that wall, and just like the runner, you will find there is usually a wonderful high on the other side.

Act

The Bible is not a philosophy or set of ideals to contemplate. It is the portal to a reality to be lived. When the Holy Spirit shows you something, believe it, trust it, and do it. We are told: "Be doers of the Word…and not merely listeners to it.…Faith, if it does not have works (deeds and actions of obedience to back it up), by itself is destitute of power (inoperative, dead)" (James 1:22; 2:17, AMP). Doing what the Spirit shows you will activate and energize your faith. You will become more sensitive and aware of the spirit realm. Over time it will become easier to access the spirit dimension, and your trust and confidence in God will grow. The apostle John tells us that as we obey God's Word to us, we grow in spiritual maturity and in intimacy with God. (See 1 John 2:5.)

Look

As you hear and do God's Word as the Holy Spirit shows it to you, look for results. Look for changes in yourself, in those around you, and in your environment. What kind of changes might you expect? You may begin to get stronger and more frequent downloads when reading the Bible. You may have times in prayer when you sense God's presence in more tangible ways, or it is easier to hear Him communicating with you. You may find Him talking more to you throughout your day. You may begin to realize that events that can seem coincidental, like running into an old friend at the store, aren't happenstance at all, but they are God-incidents. You may develop a "sixth sense" about things like when to call a friend who may need you. Sometimes you may have spiritual dreams at night or spiritual visions during the day. The more you expect to hear and act upon what you hear, the more you will have crossover experiences into the spirit realm. Life becomes an adventure. You are living in a bigger reality than just the physical dimension, and every day presents opportunities to go farther and deeper into the Spirit.

As powerful as prayer and Bible reading are in connecting you to the spirit realm, they represent two legs of your spiritual foundations. You still need a third leg to stand and not fall. Living in God's kingdom is not an isolated activity. Remember, God's desire is to be restored to relationship with His human family. The third foundation is the companionship of others who are also on their destiny voyage. Just as the starship *Enterprise* needed a crew to boldly explore the universe, we need to belong to a supportive community to encourage our spiritual growth and help keep us accountable and on track. We will look at the importance of having spiritual family in the next chapter.

⁓(**12**)ᵦ

OUT OF THE MANY, THE ONE

Although **we all** want some time to ourselves, no one really likes to be alone a lot, and none of us like being lonely. Can you remember the last time you felt lonely? Perhaps you were actually alone, but maybe you weren't. Maybe you were in a group but found yourself feeling isolated and cut off from connection with others anyway. It's kind of a sad and scary feeling all at the same time. It feels a little like being suspended in space, free floating, and unable find solid ground to stand on. You find yourself hoping the feeling won't last too long this time. Sometimes you try to distract yourself with music, TV, or going somewhere to be around people. Sometimes these distractions work and you feel better, and sometimes they don't, leaving you feeling even lonelier.

"It Is Not Good for You to Be Alone"

God did not design us to be solitary creatures. From the beginning He designed us to find our deepest fulfillment and satisfaction in relationship with others. In fact, God is the one who made the statement to Adam, "It is not good for you to be alone." He then told Adam, "I will make a helper (companion) for you." (See Genesis 2:18.) But instead of immediately creating woman, He brought all the animals for Adam to name. Adam gave them all names, but the Bible records that no suitable companion was found for Adam. It is an interesting story. I think that God wanted Adam to decide for himself what type of companion he wanted. None of the other animals were satisfactory, because none of them were in Adam's level of creation. None of them were created in the image of God like Adam.

Can you imagine Adam's delight when he awoke from the sleep God put him under and first saw woman? (By the way, woman was not called Eve until after they had sinned. Originally Adam and woman were so one, they had one name, Adam. [See Genesis 1:27.]) Now this was more like it! She was like Adam but also different in the most pleasing kind of ways! Adam immediately acknowledged their connection and kinship. He stated, "This is now bone of my bones and flesh of my flesh, she shall be called 'woman,' for she was taken out of man" (Genesis 2:23). And we know that Adam and woman shared deep companionship, because the Bible goes on to say: "The man and his wife were both naked, and they felt no shame" (Genesis 2:25). As we previously mentioned in chapter 2, this did not just refer to physical nudity but also to total transparency. Adam and woman shared everything. They knew everything about each other. They had nothing to hide or feel self-conscious about. They were equals. Neither felt inferior to the other. They had complete confidence and trust in one another. They each felt totally loved and accepted by the other.

God not only approved of their loving companionship, but He also immediately encouraged them to multiply it by having children, creating the community of family. He told them: "Be fruitful and increase in number; fill the earth and subdue it" (Genesis 1:28). God's desire was that the love Adam and woman shared would magnify and magnify as more and more people were born and populated the earth. He envisioned a human family knit together through love bonds, each encouraging and supporting one another to develop all their skills and abilities— and each using their skills and abilities to benefit the other members of the human family. It was to be an ever-widening circle of love and acceptance that would go on forever.

Personally, I think God built into us this desire and enjoyment of companionship and social connection because He is a social being. The personhood of God is a deep mystery that is beyond our finite mental capacity to grasp. The Bible is very clear that there is only one God, yet it makes reference to three distinct persons in the Godhead: the Father God, Jesus the Son, and the Holy Spirit. In some way they communicate and share companionship and love with each other, even as we do with one another. Before He was crucified, Jesus explained His relationship with the Father this way:

> The words I say to you are not just my own. Rather, it is the Father, living in me, who is doing his work. Believe me when I say that I am in the Father and the Father is in me; or at least believe on the evidence of the miracles themselves.... As the Father has loved me, so have I loved you. Now remain in my love.
> —John 14:10–11; 15:9

The heart of the Godhead is a network of relationships, a community of love. We were created in God's image, and we share His desire for and enjoyment of companionship and community.

Our success is never so sweet as when we can celebrate it with others. Pain and sadness somehow don't weigh on us quite so heavily when we know others are aware and care. We need the connection and companionship of others. Life is richer, deeper, and better when it is a shared journey. We have created a universal lifestyle of social living. From our earliest days of infancy, totally dependent and born into some type of family structure and culture, we are interacting with others, mutually giving and receiving. Most of the tasks we seek to accomplish— from sports, to building construction, to business management, to government administration, to entertainment—are group efforts. We need each other to accomplish mutually agreed-upon goals, and we must find ways to integrate our relating and efforts to make things happen. Sometimes we do this more pleasantly and effectively than others, but we still need to come together to make it happen. We do not, indeed cannot, live isolated unto ourselves.

"You Are Living Stones"

When you have an encounter with the divine ET, you begin to experience the spiritual realm. Like Neo in *The Matrix*, you begin to experience a whole new world of reality, a whole new way of thinking and being. It doesn't land on you all at once, of course, but progressively you find yourself venturing deeper and deeper into the realm of the spirit. When Neo first awoke after being deprogrammed from the Matrix, he was in a ship run by the resistance fighters. These were people who had either been deprogrammed from the Matrix, like Neo, or they were born in Zion, the freedom city outside the confines of the Matrix. They could answer his questions and share their own experiences of life outside the Matrix with him. And Neo needed their input. His world had so radically changed. He couldn't go back into the Matrix and tell his old friends. They were still plugged into the Matrix and would never understand. In fact, had he tried, Neo probably would have found his old friends would think he had flipped out. He needed to be with others who shared his current life experience. He needed their wisdom, insight, advice, and encouragement. He was able to progress much more effectively in his life outside the Matrix with the help of his friends in the resistance fighters.

Your new journey into the spirit dimension cannot be an isolated one either. You will need the companionship of others who are also on the journey. You will help one another progress and find your unique identity and destiny. You are designed and created to want connection with others and to function best within a supportive community. Life is not an individual course but a shared venture. When you said yes to the divine ET, you became part of His forever family. There is a place for you in that family where you will be accepted, encouraged, and challenged to become everything you were truly created to be.

The apostle Peter, one of Jesus's original disciples, encouraged the followers of Jesus to actively associate with and support one another. He said, "You also, like living stones, are being built up into a spiritual house" (1 Peter 2:5). In Hebrews 10:24–25, the writer states: "And let us consider how we may spur one another on toward love and good deeds. Let us not give up meeting together, as some are in the habit of doing, but let us encourage one another." And the apostle Paul wrote extensively in 1 Corinthians about the family of God, referring to it as the body of Jesus Christ. He noted that our physical bodies are made up of many different parts, each serving different functions, that are integrated together. In the same way, the body of Jesus contains many different parts (people) with different skills and abilities, which provide different functions. What each person brings is valuable and needed, and all must work together if the body is to progress and grow in spiritual power and authority.

Jesus's followers of long ago were simply stating what we

know is a universal truth: We need one another to accomplish goals. We need to support and mutually encourage one another on our respective life journeys. We need the wisdom and skills that others share with us. The more we come together in a spirit of harmony and caring, the more we all grow and progress. Truly out of the combined efforts of many, each one of us flourishes. As the apostle Peter put it, "You are living stones." Alone, each stone remains just that, a stone. But together they can become a structure and serve a purpose they could never attain to if they remained isolated and individual stones.

"A Threefold Cord Is Not Easily Broken"

If you are like most people, individual relationships are what mean the most to you and have the greatest impact on your life. In one sense, any community is the product of a network of individual relationships. Have you ever heard the saying, "A threefold cord is not easily broken"? The saying is actually from the Bible, Ecclesiastes 4:12, and it reads:

> Though one may be overpowered,
>   two can defend themselves.
> A cord of three strands is not quickly broken.

What does it mean? I used to think that it meant there is safety in numbers. You know you are stronger if someone else joins forces with you. Of course that is true, but that would be a twofold cord. Why does it specify a threefold cord?

I now think it is a threefold cord because God is the third party in the relationship between the two people. When followers of Jesus form friendships, they have the automatic presence of God the Holy Spirit in the middle of their relating. That creates a threefold cord, a strong friendship that is not easily broken. The presence of the Holy Spirit changes the type of connection and commitment that followers of Jesus make with one another. The Bible provides various descriptions of this type of relationship. In Proverbs 18:24 it states, "There is a friend who sticks closer than a brother." While we all hope that we are close to our siblings and relatives, that is not always the case. But between two followers of Jesus there can be a connection that is stronger than that between two siblings.

Again, in Proverbs 17:17 it is written, "A friend loves at all times, and a brother is born for adversity." A true friend is not a fair-weather one. A true friend will hang in there with you when times are tough. You know you can handle more when you have an ally by your side. Beyond that, in the spirit dimension, your power is increased tenfold when you have another follower of Jesus stand with you. The Bible says that one can put a thousand to flight, but two can put ten thousand to flight. (See Deuteronomy 32:30.)

A true friend will care enough for you to be honest no matter what. When they speak either praise or criticism, you know you can believe it. They are sharing the truth with you from a heart of love and a desire to see you grow and progress. When it is sincere, it is, "Oil and perfume rejoice the heart; so does the sweetness of a friend's counsel that comes from the heart" (Proverbs 27:9, AMP). It feels good because you know your friend is sharing his or her real heart with you. Even when a friend needs to tell you something about yourself that is not so complimentary, you can receive it because you know your friend wouldn't say something in petty anger just to hurt you and tear you down. Proverbs 27:6 says, "Faithful are the wounds of a friend" (NKJV). And Proverbs 27:17 says, "As iron sharpens iron, so a man sharpens the countenance of his friend" (NKJV).

This quality of friendship doesn't grow on trees, but it is the type of friendship to which God calls us as followers of Jesus. Will any of us do it perfectly? The obvious answer is no. But we do have a divine ally—the Holy Spirit, who will enable us to grow in our ability to be a true friend. We simply need to invite Him to help us and follow His directives. I think it's also important for you to know that God not only wants you to become a friend like this, but He also wants you to have friends like this. He is the one who stated, "It is not good for you to be alone," and He is the one who will provide you with real friendships that last and can be trusted. He knows that you need companions on your destiny journey. He also knows that you become like those with whom you hang out. Make it your aim to hang out with friends who pull the highest and best out of you. Talk to God in prayer about finding this type of friends and your desires for companionship. He has promised that if we ask Him for something that is in agreement with His will and purpose, He will give us what we ask for. God wants you to have real friends, so ask Him!

life Signs

Individual friendships are one of the most important relationships we have on our journey in the spirit dimension. They bring us joy and provide encouragement and comfort; when needed, they challenge us. They are the people with whom we can most "be ourselves" without fear of rejection or reprisal. But they are not the only relationships we require on our destiny journey. We also need to relate to a larger network of people, a community. The community contains collective wisdom and resources that go beyond what the individual friendship can provide. The community can provide us with a variety of perspectives and the opportunity to learn skills not available in the friendship. The community can also provide additional support during tough times and hold us accountable when we need to take responsibility for our own growth. An individual friendship cannot supply all these needs.

As we broaden our circle and allow more people to have some significance, we of course run the risk that we will be let down and disappointed by some people. While we can handpick our individual friends, we cannot handpick all the members of any community group we may choose to join. I wish I could tell you that followers of Jesus never do hurtful and unkind things to one another. Of course, that is not the truth. Any community will be made of imperfect people, each of them on their individual destiny voyage and all of them at different stages of growth and maturity. Some of them will hurt and disappoint you. And let's be real. Some of them you will hurt and disappoint, too. Part of acquiring power and authority in the spirit dimension is learning how to avoid taking everything personally. It is also recognizing our own imperfections and taking responsibility for the difficulties we may cause others. This requires courage and strength of character. It is always much easier to resort to anger and blame shifting. Again, the spirit realm is no place for wimps!

What am I referring to when I use the term *community*? Basically I am talking about a group of people who are committed to following Jesus. Usually they are organized into some type of structure like a church that provides an identified time and place to come together. They gather together to share experiences on their spiritual journey, to praise and thank God, to pray, and to hear training or teaching from the Bible. They will often have various social activities and opportunities to simply enjoy being together. Frequently they join their efforts to help in various projects to the outside community and even get involved in service programs in other countries.

If the word *church* is a big turnoff for you, I can't say that I blame you. Perhaps you have stayed away from the Bible and church for years because of negative experiences that you've had with Bible-thumping, churchgoing people. If so, I can see why you wouldn't be too anxious to expose yourself to that again. But I hope you are willing to consider this fact: just because you may have had a run-in with someone who was a hypocrite or perhaps simply immature and overly zealous doesn't mean you have experienced what a truly alive church is like. And you will never know for sure unless you risk another exposure.

While I can't insure you will have error-free selection, I would like to offer some recommendations on how to find an "alive" church. When I use the term *alive*, I mean a church where people are serious about following Jesus and learning to walk in the spirit dimension. They are not simply being religious. Just like in Jesus's time, there are people today who have all the outward trappings of religion but have never had an encounter with the divine ET or entered into the spirit dimension. You will want to avoid them. They have nothing to offer you.

Look for these "life signs" when selecting a community to which to belong:

Does it look like a family?

If you were to go to a major family reunion, you would see people of all ages and at all stages of life. Healthy families don't just associate with the members who look and act like them. They mix and mingle with one another, and every member is valued. You want to be part of a community where you can learn from members representing a variety of ages and stages in life. Since this is a family of God, it should contain the same type of cultural, racial, and ethnic diversity as the city where it is located. If the community is too homogenous, it may lack sufficient diversity and breadth to provide the collective wisdom and resources you may need. Note this has nothing to do with community size. Fairly small communities may be quite diversified, while large communities may vary little.

Does it act like a family?

How do people treat one another? Do they seem to recognize, know, and enjoy each other? What is the "warmth level"? Just as you can pick up the family atmosphere in someone's home, you can pick up the family atmosphere in a church. Does the atmosphere feel friendly and personable, or cold and distant? Watch what people do, not what the environment looks like. Attractive surroundings are always a plus, but you can have designer churches, just as there are designer homes. The shell looks great, but there is no substance.

How are you welcomed . . . or are you?

You are new. If the community values new members, it should have some way established to identify you and help you feel at home. Do people around you greet you? At some point does anyone in leadership notice and welcome you? Does anyone tell you about the community? If so, what do they say, and do they seem to mean it? Are you given any information about the church and invited back? Does anyone take time to find out who you are and gather information about your journey and your interests? Is it someplace that feels like home to you? Would you like to go back?

What is the church about?

Some churches do little more than gather once a week. Real communities spend more time together. What other types of activities is the community committed to during the week? Most churches have some type of bulletin or information brochure. Take a look at it. Are there opportunities to gather in smaller groups to share experiences, pray together, receive training, study the Bible, or get involved in service projects outside the church? Does it look like the community ever socializes together in any ways other than coffee on Sunday morning? Talk to a few people. Why did they join this community? What are they about? If you like what you see and hear, try out a couple of the other activities during the week to see if your positive impressions hold up.

Is the church spiritually alive?

I can guarantee that if the above four life signs are not present, you will not want to stay and get involved in the community. If this life sign is not present, I'd advise you to leave, even if the above four life signs are all there. If this life sign is absent, you are in a religious social club, not necessarily a community of people dedicated to following Jesus.

What is emphasized? Do you hear Jesus being referred to? Do people talk about Jesus as if He is someone they know personally? Do people talk about the Holy Spirit and being guided by the Spirit? Does there seem to be an emphasis on being filled with the Spirit? Is this a praying community? Do people pray openly with each other? Is there a time of corporate prayer or an opportunity for people to receive additional prayer after the service or at some other time during the week? Is God's Word important? Do most people bring their Bibles to church? When the leader makes a reference to a specific section of the Bible, do people turn to it and follow along? Do people talk about God's Word in their conversations with each other?

Is there a time of thanksgiving and praise to God? Most often this is expressed in some type of music and singing, but it also can be people sharing personal experiences. Do people seem to be enthusiastically caught up in thanksgiving and praise or just going through the motions? Do you hear any references to kingdom living or spiritual authority and power? Do the people and the leadership expect that unusual things like miracles can and should happen to them alone and together? Do they have an organized way to pray for the sick and those with other needs? Are there regular reports of answers to those prayers, such as people getting healed or getting jobs, promotions, or relationships being restored (like a marriage being put back together)? Are they excited about what they hear God telling them today? Do they hear new words from God? Do they believe that God is still speaking today to individuals? Do they share personal encounters with God? Is there transparency in relating? Are people conversing about significant subjects with candor and apparent honesty? Do people seem genuinely concerned and caring with each other? Do they take time to interact and speak words of encouragement to one another? Do all types of people attend and seem comfortable and equally welcome?

Is there an interest and passion for sharing the good news about the kingdom of God and the love of Jesus with others, especially those outside the community? Is there an interest and involvement in spreading this good news to foreign countries? Does this community have strong positive ties to other communities in the local area and elsewhere?

I sincerely believe that a community that is spiritually alive will exhibit the other four life signs as well. When you find a community that is spiritually alive, join it! Get involved, and see what opens up to you. This is an excellent place to meet new friends. For some of you, such a community will become the loving family you may never have had. It will most certainly provide a solid and safe place in which you can learn more about living in the spirit dimension. God uses His family to encourage and build each other up. Although just a small glimpse, this family is God's way of allowing all of us to experience something of heaven here on Earth. Being part of a spiritually alive community brushes each of us up against our destiny as beings from another reality, a larger, spiritual one.

Remember, your destiny journey is not a solo voyage. Intimate relationship is at the heart of the universe. God intends for you to have the deep satisfaction of true companionship and the stability of being part of a community, His family. He wants you to be able to share your triumphs and challenges, receive support and encouragement, and have access to wise counsel and guidance. He created you in such a way that you will discover your identity and destiny in the company of fellow sojourners. He desires that your destiny journey be a rich, full, joyous, and deeply shared experience. Jesus expressed this desire so well when He stated, "I am come that they [that is, *all* of us] might have life, and that they might have it more abundantly" (John 10:10, KJV).

(epilogue)

THE HIDDEN MYSTERY
BEFORE All WORLDS BEGAN

This book has been quite a journey. I want to thank you for taking it with me. I hope you have opened yourself to an actual encounter with the divine ET. If you have, I know you have experienced something that no words, no matter how well crafted, can ever capture. In some way that you may not even be able to articulate, you have become aware of the reality of the divine ET and His incredible love for you. You have touched the larger reality of the spirit dimension and are beginning to understand how limited life in only the physical dimension is. Your way of thinking and being in the world is in transformation, and you can now contain thoughts and understandings that a short time ago would have seemed very strange and even fantastic.

I've only been able to touch upon how to continue to grow and progress as you walk in the spirit dimension. I hope you will become a sincere God seeker and follower your entire life. I encourage you to make Bible reading and prayer time with God a daily habit. And I strongly urge you to find a spiritually alive community and become a part of it. Your life will continue to transform as you do. Believe me, the wonders are just beginning to unfold for you. First Corinthians 2:9 says, "Eye has not seen, nor ear heard, nor have entered into the heart of man the things which God has prepared for those who love Him" (NKJV).

You are now part of the fulfillment of God's dream. From before the universe exploded into existence, God had a dream. It was a hidden mystery before all worlds began—a mystery so deep and so expansive that no one but God could fathom it. We've talked about God's deep desire for a human family to love and be loved by. We know that God is relational and desires relationship with us. But do you know why? This is the mystery He's kept hidden for so long. He desires this intimate union and love communion with His human family so that through that love relating He can make Himself, in all His infinite variety, known. He wants to lay everything He is and has before the entire universe by demonstrating it through His love for us! And by saying yes to an encounter with Him, you have opened yourself to this destiny in and with Him!

I wish I could explain it better, but I know the mystery is

far beyond my comprehension, let alone my meager words. But it is our joint destiny voyage. It is a journey straight into the very heart of God, to be flooded with the essence of His being, His never-ending love for us. It is clearly an adventure larger than any life we know and completely out of this, or any, world. And it has barely begun. The best by far is yet to come!

⤳(notes)⤳

❙ We Are Not Alone

1. *Close Encounters of the Third Kind*, directed by Steven Spielberg (Culver City, CA: Columbia Pictures Corporation, 1977).

2. Steven J. Dick, *Life on Other Worlds: The Twentieth Century Extraterrestrial Life Debate* (New York: Cambridge University Press, 1998), xiii.

3. Erich von Daniken, *Chariots of the Gods* (New York: G.P. Putnam's Sons, 1969).

4. Gregory S. Paul, "Cross National Correlations of Quantifiable Societal Health with Popular Religiosity and Secularism in the Prosperous Democracies," *Journal of Religion and Society* 7 (2005): 2005–2011.

5. Wikipedia.org, s.v. "Geiger-Marsden Experiment," http://en.wikipedia.org/wiki/Geiger-Marsden_experiment (accessed February 14, 2007).

6. Wikipedia.org, s.v. "Francesco Redi," http://en.wikipedia .org/wiki/Francesco_Redi (accessed February 14, 2007).

7. Wikipedia.org, s.v. "Anti-Gravity," http://en.wikipedia.org/ wiki/Anti-gravity (accessed February 14, 2007).

8. Wikipedia.org, s.v. "Edwin Hubble," http://en.wikipedia.org/ wiki/Edwin_Hubble (accessed February 14, 2007).

9. Hazel Muir, "Universe Might Yet Collapse in 'Big Crunch,'" NewScientist.com, September 6, 2002, http://www .newscientist.com/article.ns?id=dn2759 (accessed February 14, 2007).

10. Wikipedia.org, s.v. "Archibald Sayce," http://en.wikipedia .org/wiki/Archibald_Sayce (accessed March 21, 2007).

11. Hugh Ross, "Fulfilled Prophecy: Evidence for the Reliability of the Bible," *The Skeptical Review*, January/February 1996, Infidels.org, http://www.infidels.org/library/magazines/ tsr/1996/1/1ross96.html (accessed February 15, 2007).

12. *Contact*, directed by Robert Zemeckis (Burbank, CA: Warner Bros., 1997), accessed via "The Truth," Turning-Pages.com, http://www.turning-pages.com/contact/truth .htm (accessed January 25, 2007).

2 First Contact: The Eden Dimension

1. The Bible versions that I will use in this book in addition to the NIV will be referred to by these abbreviations: KJV, the King James Version of the Bible; NKJV, the New King James Version of the Bible (replaces "thee," "thou," "shall," and the like); and AMP, the Amplified Bible.

3 Paradise Lost

1. "Morpheus' Proposal," *The Matrix*, DVD, directed by Andy Wachowski and Larry Wachowski (1999; Burbank, CA: Warner Home Video, 1999).

2. "The Search Is Over," *The Matrix*, DVD.

3. "The Gatekeepers," *The Matrix*, DVD.

4. "The Oracle," *The Matrix Reloaded*, DVD, directed by Andy Wachowski and Larry Wachowski (2003; Burbank, CA: Warner Home Video, 2003).

5. "The Real World," *The Matrix*, DVD.

6. Ibid.

4 Alien Battle Lines

1. Wikipedia.org, s.v. "Orson Welles," http://en.wikipedia.org/wiki/Orson_Welles (accessed February 15, 2007).

6 Love Is Not a Four-Letter Word

1. *Star Wars IV: A New Hope*, directed by George Lucas (Los Angeles, CA: Twentieth-Century Fox Film Corporation, 1977).

7 The Divine Sting: The Mystery of the Ages Revealed

1. "Neo's Choice," *The Matrix Revolutions*, DVD, directed by Andy Wachowski and Larry Wachowski (2003; Burbank, CA: Warner Home Video, 2004).

2. "Inevitable and Over," *The Matrix Revolutions*, DVD.

3. Ibid.

8 Encounter With the Divine ET: The Red Pill or the Blue Pill

1. "The Rabbit Hole," *The Matrix*, DVD.

9 The Force Is With You

1. To read the actual account of this story, see Joy Dawson, *Intercession, Thrilling and Fulfilling* (Seattle, WA: YWAM Publishing, 1997), 27–28.

2. "Day by Day" written by Stephen Schwartz. Used by permission of Range Road Music Inc. on behalf of itself and New Cadenza Music Corp. Used by permission of co-publisher Hal Leonard Corporation.

10 To Boldly Go Where You Have Never Been Before

1. Wikipedia.org, s.v. "Where No Man Has Gone Before," http://en.wikipedia.org/wiki/Where_no_man_has_gone_before (accessed February 7, 2007).

2. *E.T. the Extra-Terrestrial*, directed by Steven Spielberg (Universal City, CA: Universal Pictures, 1982).

11 The User's Manual for Another Reality

1. "Nebuchadnezzar's Crew," *The Matrix*, DVD.

2. "The Real World," *The Matrix*, DVD.